SACRAMENTO PUBLIC LIBRARY

3 3029 03956 2525

SOUTH NATOMAS LIBRARY
1620 WEST EL CAMINO AVENUE
SACRAMENTO, CA 95833
OCT 13, 1998

MAR   2009 14

WITHDRAWN FROM COLLECTION
OF SACRAMENTO PUBLIC LIBRARY

D1165238

Carol Endler Sterbenz

At Home
for Christmas

Carol Endler Sterbenz

At Home for Christmas

Selected by Carol Endler Sterbenz and the Editors of *Handcraft Illustrated*

Reader's Digest

The Reader's Digest Association, Inc.
Pleasantville, New York/Montreal

A Reader's Digest Book

Conceived and edited by the Editors of *Handcraft Illustrated*
Designed by Elaine Hackney

Copyright © 1998 Boston Common Press Inc.
All rights reserved. Unauthorized reproduction, in any manner, is prohibited.

The credits that appear on page 190 are hereby made a part of this copyright page.

Library of Congress Cataloging in Publication Data
Sterbenz, Carol Endler.
Carol Sterbenz at home for Christmas / by the editors of Handcraft Illustrated.
p.   cm.—(Fast and fabulous)
Includes index.
ISBN 0-7621-0094-X
1. Christmas decorations. 2. Handicraft. I Reader's Digest Association.
II. Handcraft illustrated. III. Title. IV. Series
TT900.C4S726   1998   98-5960
745.594'12—dc21

Reader's Digest and the Pegasus logo are registered trademarks of The Reader's Digest Association, Inc.
Printed in the United States of America

Introduction

It begins with a feeling, a subtle sense of visiting the past and a desire to keep the nostalgia alive. I remember my mother teaching my sisters and me how to make woven paper hearts from shiny colored paper. Last Christmas I was given a slender box, unadorned except for a handwritten card in my mother's handwriting, "For Carol." I lifted the lid and in an instant I was young again, fiddling with paper strips, weaving them into heart-shaped envelopes, each to become a small pouch for candy. My mother collected several of the heart baskets I had made when I was a child, thinking it would be the perfect gift now that I had a family of my own and children who were old enough to continue the tradition of making these little paper baskets.

The memories of the fun my sisters and I had when making those paper hearts, the stories we told each other, my mother's guiding hands—all these things inspired me to continue the family tradition of making heart baskets, this symbol of love, with my own three children years later. Of course, we also began traditions of our own, activities that we continue to do together today, despite the changes that time and circumstances have brought. We always make gingerbread houses, each child decorating an entire side, a custom that has evolved with the children's ages, developing skills, and diverging tastes.

It is traditions like these that make Christmas my favorite time of the year; at no other time is our family so filled with the spirit of being together and making things. There is nothing more pleasurable, and that is the spirit in which this book was written.

Thanks to our editors and writers, I'm proud to present a wonderful collection of handmade projects that, with your special touches, symbolize the heart and soul of Christmas. The first three chapters in the book—Wreaths, Ornaments, and Mantel Decorations—include a wide range of projects for creating a personal, welcoming, festive atmosphere at home. I hope they will inspire you to start holiday traditions of your very own. In sumptuous and inspiring photographs, you will get a close-up view of all manner of decoration—an elegantly classic silk rose wreath greets you at the front door; a tree boughs bend with exquisite ornaments made of beads; a mantel is decked with stockings, a charming sparkling village, and a unique stocking that stands up on its own.

The last two chapters—Greeting Cards and Gift Tags, and Handmade Gifts—provide many ideas for conveying your sentiments to friends and family through hand-fashioned gifts and personalized cards, including bath oil, velvet pouches, beaded votives, and even a few charming toys for the youngest person on your gift list.

The beauty and sophistication of every project belies the simple techniques and materials required to make it. We've tested each project and devised techniques to streamline the step-by-step process of creating it. Everything included in this book is readily adaptable to your own taste, quick to make up, and truly accessible to crafters of all levels. We provide everything you need to know to make the projects, but leave the personal touches up to you. These are the special details that speak to your friends and family of your thoughtfulness, that give every tradition meaning and every gift its heart.

With all good wishes for a joyous holiday,

Carol Endler Sterbenz
Editor, Handcraft Illustrated

Contents

Wreaths

White Rose Wreath   10

Empire-Style Door Wreath   14

Della Robbia Wreath   18

Evergreen, Rose, & Lime Wreath   22

Reversible Table Wreath   26

Ornaments

Trio of Glass Balls   32

Embossed Tree Ornaments   38

Glitter Balls   44

Crystal and Wire Ornaments   48

Beaded Star Ornaments   52

Moravian Glitter Stars   58

Glitter Fruit   62

Keepsake Silver Bird Ornament   68

Mantel Decorations

Hinged Angel Screen   74

Appliquéd Wool Stocking   78

Cuffed Velvet Stocking   84

Gilded Glitter Village   88

Gilded Candles   94

Gingerbread Birdhouses   98

Court Jester Stocking   104

Greeting Cards and Gift Tags

Cut-Window Collage Cards   112

Folded Paper Envelopes   116

Scotty Dog Holiday Card   120

Laminated Greeting Cards   124

Stationery Greeting Cards   128

Rubber Stamp Gift Tags   132

Handmade Gifts

Bath Oil   138

Miniature Notepad Books   142

Meringue Mushrooms   146

Pavé Box   150

Zippered Suede Purses   154

Lined Velvet Pouches   158

Faux Brushed-Steel Frame   162

Beaded Votive Candle Holder   166

Custom-Fit Teddy Bear Sweaters   170

Terry Cloth Bunny and Piglet   174

Appendix

Patterns   180-187   Sources   188

Credits   190   Index   191

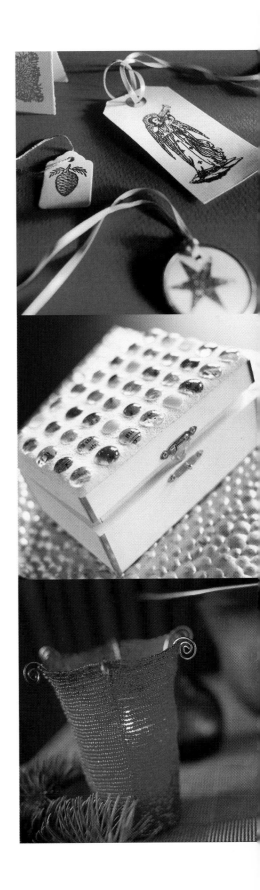

Wreaths

 The wreath is one of the most

enduring and versatile decorations

at holiday time—be it large

or small; round or square; ornate or simple; fresh,

dried, or artificial. Hung on the front door

or in a window, a wreath is a welcoming beacon.

In this chapter, you'll find several easy

techniques for making and displaying wreaths.

These methods provide ready-made

designs for you to follow or a point of departure from

which you can create your own designs.

White Rose Wreath

White roses are a most elegant flower, and this silk flower

wreath is a holiday celebration of their beauty.

The method for making the wreath is simple: Wire artificial

rose blooms to a wire wreath base, concealing

the stems and most of the leaves as you go. To finish the

wreath, you'll wire on red berries. The real

challenge here is aesthetic: to add visual interest to the

monochromatic design while maintaining a

bountiful and natural look. By selecting different size blooms,

measuring between 3in and 5in (7.5cm and 12.5cm)

across, you can add lifelike texture and avoid the monotony

and flatness that might occur if you use

roses of the same size.

Materials

Yields one 24in (60.1cm)-diameter wreath

- 50–70 assorted white silk roses
- 10–15 sprigs small artificial red holly berries
- 7–10 sprigs large artificial burgundy mulberries
- 20in (51cm)-diameter wire wreath base
- 30-gauge green florist's wire

YOU'LL ALSO NEED:
wire cutters and ruler.

Instructions

1. *Prepare roses.* Using wire cutters, trim each rose stem to 12in (30.5cm). Sort roses by size in separate piles.

2. *Join roses to wreath base.* Lay wire wreath base face up on flat surface. Weave one rose stem under one spoke and over adjacent spoke, pulling it through until flower rests on top (see illustration A, facing page). Select a different size rose, insert its stem next to first rose, then weave stem onto form in same way. Continue adding new roses over woven stems. As you add roses to wreath, conceal leaves as much as possible. Too many leaves along edges imparts a funereal wreath look. But don't cut leaves off, as they add body to wreath even though you can't see them.

3. *Fill out wreath.* Weave all stems in the same direction, working from side to side for full, even coverage as you proceed around wreath. Poke leaves through to underside as much as possible (illustration B). As you come full circle, it may be necessary to weave new stems through

THE HISTORY OF WREATHS

Wreath making is an ancient craft. They are significant for their connection to holidays and historical events and because of the supposed properties of the herbs they are made from. Their circular shape is symbolic of continual life. In the busy market places of ancient Greece and Rome, wreaths were generously available and sought after for many reasons. They were used to soothe the heads of those who were reveling too late into the night, to bring wisdom and memory to the scholar, and to bring luck to the lover. During the festival of Saturnalia, Romans decorated their homes with evergreens to symbolize life and rebirth.

Wreaths were also used as crowns of glory, given as prizes to honor success and achievement. Olive wreaths were given to winners of the Greek games at Panathenaia and Olympia. Oak leaves were given to war heroes and statesmen, and artists and poets wore ivy.

In medieval artwork, wreaths crown the heads of the Virgin Mary and the saints. In the monasteries, monks cultivated herbs and other plants, many of which became associated with certain saints because they were plentiful during the feast days when the saints were honored. The plants were also used to make garlands and wreaths for religious festivals and celebrations.

already-woven stems instead of wreath base. Use remaining roses to fill
out wreath where needed.

4. ***Add berries to wreath.*** Attach large burgundy mulberries first,
then small red holly berries. Arrange berry sprigs on front of wreath at
random, and anchor with florist's wire from the back (illustration C).

Weaving the Roses

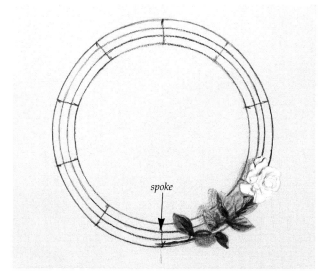

A. Weave a single rose stem onto a wire wreath base.

B. Work in new roses, covering the existing stems.

C. Accent the finished wreath with sprigs of berries.

 *Wreaths*

Empire-Style Door Wreath

During the busy holiday season,

the ideal door wreath looks regal, is easy to assemble,

and uses materials that are readily available.

This classic wreath meets all three criteria. You'll need only

one type of foliage—fresh lemon leaves,

which can be purchased by the branch in floral shops—

to cover the ready-made straw wreath base.

Begin by painting half of the leaves gold, then pin the lemon

leaves to the wreath with florist's pins.

Materials

Yields one 18in (46cm)-diameter wreath

- 550–600 fresh lemon leaves
- 18in (46cm)-diameter straw wreath base
- 4½yds (4m) 2¾in (7cm)-wide green velvet wire-edged ribbon
- 1yd (1m) gold metallic twisted cord
- Bright gold metallic spray paint
- 10–15 white plastic 13gal (52L) trash bags
- 30-gauge green spool wire
- Florist's pins

YOU'LL ALSO NEED:

newspaper; wire cutters; scotch tape; permanent marker; and scissors.

designer's tip
✳ ✳ ✳ ✳ ✳ ✳ ✳
Instead of painting half the lemon leaves, gold substitute another metallic color, such as silver, copper, or bronze, then use matching cord when decorating the wreath.

Instructions

1. *Paint leaves gold.* Spread out newspaper in well-ventilated work area. Lay approximately 300 lemon leaves face up on newspaper and spray with gold metallic paint following manufacturer's instructions. Let dry at least one hour, preferably overnight, before handling.

2. *Wrap and mark wreath.* Wrap plastic bag around wreath, concealing straw. Tape bags in place as you go for temporary hold. Continue wrapping wreath with second bag, winding in same direction (see illustration A, facing page), until all straw is concealed. Add one or two more bag layers to build up wreath bulk. Bind entire wreath with wire to secure bags permanently. Visualizing wreath as a clock face, use permanent marker to draw lines at 2, 5, 6, 7, 10, and 12 o'clock positions (illustration B) for leaf placement.

3. *Pin leaves to wreath in tiers.* Position several gold leaves horizontally across 6 o'clock line; to secure, push florist's pins through leaf tips. Repeat to cover entire 6 o'clock line. Working toward right, position next tier of gold leaves across wreath so lower tips overlap and conceal previously inserted pins; secure with pins. Repeat to attach two or three additional tiers, or enough to conceal 5 o'clock line (illustration C). Each tier should conceal previous tier's pins. Repeat to add gold tiers up left side to reach 7 o'clock line. Pin approximately ten tiers of green leaves up each side to reach 2 and 10 o'clock lines (illustration D). Finish with about seven tiers of gold leaves on each side to reach 12 o'clock line.

4. *Add ribbon and cord.* To finish, wrap green ribbon around wreath at 12 o'clock position and tie into four-loop bow. Shape streamers to dangle into center of wreath and notch ends. Loop gold cord into 4in (10cm)-diameter circle with two 12in (30.5cm)-long streamers; knot ends to prevent raveling and wire to bow knot.

Building up a Wreath Form

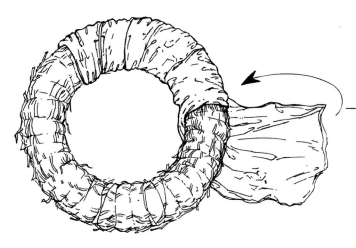

A. Wrap a wreath base with plastic bags.

B. Mark the wreath for leaf placement.

Covering Wreath with Leaves

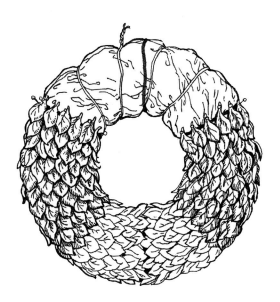

C. Attach gold lemon leaves in tiers with florist's pins.

D. Continue pinning leaves up the sides of the wreath.

Della Robbia Wreath

This wreath conveys the abundance

and festivity of the holiday season using bouquets

of artificial fruit and silk foliage.

You'll need a wire wreath base to support the

weight of the bouquets, which you

assemble from foliage sprays, sprigs of artificial

berries, and a variety of other wired

artificial fruit, then lash them to the wreath base

using 18-gauge florist's wire.

Materials

- 20 sprigs artificial berries
- 4 pine cones
- 3 artificial cherries
- 4-6 red and yellow artificial apples
- 2 miniature artificial oranges
- 4-6 miniature artificial pears
- 2 miniature artificial pomegranates
- 4 artificial strawberries
- 6–10 other artificial fruits
- 10 sprays silk foliage
- 8in (20.5cm)-diameter wire wreath base
- flat spools of 18- and 30-gauge florist's wire

YOU'LL ALSO NEED:
pruning shears; and needle-nose pliers.

designer's tip
✳ ✳ ✳ ✳ ✳ ✳ ✳
Using prepared bouquets, with a set number and type of plants per bouquet, creates a design with a uniform pattern. Bands of color can be mapped out by alternating between bouquets of different plants.

Instructions

1. *Wire pine cones.* Cut 6in (15cm) lengths of 30-gauge wire as needed to wire pine cones. See below for instructions.

2. *Make and bind bouquets.* Make ten bouquets, each containing one foliage spray, two sprigs of berries, and two fruits from materials list; keep back of bouquet flat. Bind stems with 30-gauge wire, then conceal wire with florist's tape (see illustration D, facing page). Clip off ends, leaving 2in (5cm) stem (illustration E).

3. *Bind bouquets to wreath.* Using 18-gauge wire, bind bouquets to wreath base, filling in bare spaces with single stems of fruit or foliage. Begin as follows: Attach wire to wreath base by wrapping tightly several times around one spoke. (The flat spool of wire can be turned sideways to fit between the metal prongs on the wire wreath base.) Lay one bouquet on base, flat side down and facing wreath center. Wind wire around stem and wreath base several times (illustration F). Hold wire steady. Lay second bouquet on base so it faces out and stems cross. Resume winding wire to secure stem of second bouquet (illustration G). Add third bouquet, facing in, and bind to base. Continue adding bouquets, alternating their direction, to fill front of wreath all around. To add final bouquet, slip its stem under head of first bouquet and bind it securely. To end off, anchor wire to spoke and clip off excess (illustration H).

4. *Attach pine cones with wire.* Using 18-gauge wire, attach pine cones as desired.

WIRING A PINE CONE INVISIBLY

A. Cut 6in (15cm) length of 30-gauge wire. Wrap the wire around the cone, concealing it between the scales, until it comes full cir-

B. Using needle-nose pliers, twist the wire ends together for ½in (12mm).

C. Bend the twisted wire stem down.

Making the Bouquets

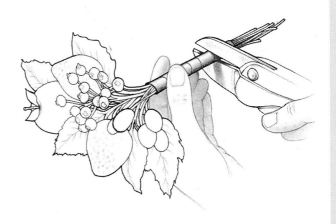

D. Assemble the foliage, berries, and fruit into a bouquet. Bind the stems with wire, then conceal them with florist's tape.

E. Clip off the ends, leaving a small stem.

Binding the Bouquets

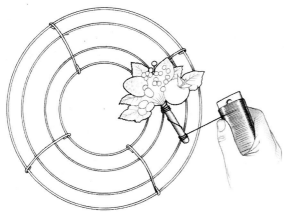

F. Secure the wire to the base, then wind it around the stem.

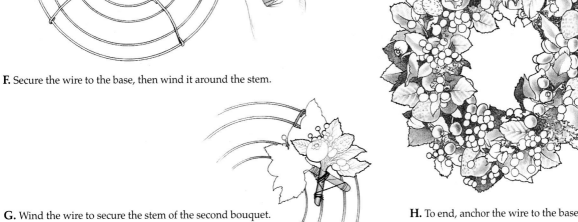

G. Wind the wire to secure the stem of the second bouquet.

H. To end, anchor the wire to the base.

Evergreen, Rose & Lime Wreath

This wreath, with its array of fresh winter foliage, fruit,

and flowers, is a beautiful and fragrant way

to welcome guests. It is also quick to make, thanks to

a simple technique of binding bouquets of

decorative materials to a ready-made wreath base. As the

wreath and binding material must be able

to support the decorative material, you'll need a sturdy

straw wreath base to hold the heavy weight

and girth of the greenery and 30-gauge florist's wire

to bind the materials to the wreath.

To enhance the longevity of the foliage, condition it after

binding in bunches but before lashing to the

wreath (see "Keeping Fresh Foliage Hydrated," page 24).

Materials

- *Forty 7in (18cm) sprigs fresh juniper*
- *Forty 7in (18cm) sprigs fresh fir*
- *Forty 7in (18cm) sprigs fresh euonymus*
- *Forty 7in (18cm) sprigs fresh blue spruce*
- *Forty 7in (18cm) sprigs privet hedge*
- *6 cream-colored roses with 7in (18cm) stems*
- *4 whole limes*
- *6 orchid vials*
- *10in (25.5cm)-diameter straw wreath base*
- *30-gauge florist's wire*
- *Florist's tape*

YOU'LL ALSO NEED:

sharp kitchen knife; and pruning shears.

Instructions

1. *Make bouquets.* Make forty bouquets, each containing a sprig of juniper, fir, euonymus, spruce, and privet hedge (see illustration A, facing page); keep back of bouquet flat. Bind stems with florist's wire, then conceal wire with florist's tape (illustration B). Clip off ends, leaving 2in (5cm) stem (illustration C).

2. *Prepare limes and roses.* Cut twenty slices of lime, each ⅜in (9mm) thick. Thread 10in (25.5cm) length wire through each slice near rind and twist to secure. Insert rose stems into vials filled with water. Set wired limes and rose stems aside.

3. *Bind bouquets to wreath base.* Bind bouquets to wreath base, filling in bare spaces with single stems of foliage. Attach wire to wreath base by wrapping tightly several times around wreath base. Lay one bouquet on base, flat side down and facing wreath center. Wind wire around stem and wreath base several times (illustration D). Hold wire steady. Lay second bouquet on base so it faces out and stems cross. Resume winding wire to secure stem of second bouquet (illustration E). Add third bouquet, facing in, and bind to base. Continue adding bouquets, alternating their direction, to fill front of wreath all around. To add final bouquet, slip its stem under head of first bouquet and bind it securely. To end off, anchor wire to spoke and clip off excess (illustration F).

4. *Finish wreath.* Wire on lime slices and insert vials into straw as shown in photograph on page 22. When you hang the wreath, be sure that you don't hang the wreath in direct sunlight.

KEEPING FRESH FOLIAGE HYDRATED

Wreaths, made from fresh plants with woody stems, need water to stay fresh-looking. Here are two ways to counteract dehydration:

- Put stems in a bucket of water before making them into bouquets to bind to the wreath. Cut the stems of the plants diagonally 1 in (2.5cm) from the bottom, then immerse the stems in a mixture of water and floral food for several hours. Commercially prepared floral foods provide the plant with nutrients and discourage the growth of bacteria that eventually rots the plant.
- Lightly mist the leaves with water once you have bound the foliage into a wreath. Repeat once a day for up to two weeks.

Making the Bouquets

A. Make forty bouquets, each containing a sprig of juniper, fir, euonymus, spruce, and privet hedge.

B. Assemble the foliage into a bouquet. Bind the stems with wire, then conceal them with tape.

C. Clip off the ends, leaving a small stem.

Binding the Bouquets

D. Tie the wire to the base, then wind it around the stem.

E. Wind the wire to secure the stem of the second bouquet.

F. To end, anchor the wire to the base.

Reversible Table Wreath

This wreath, designed for viewing from

either side, can be used in place of a centerpiece on a table.

A wreath this size (7½in [20cm] in diameter)

requires foliage in proportion—leaves about ½in (12mm) long.

The leaves should also be visually appealing

fresh or dried, as this wreath does not contain a water supply,

such as water-soaked foam. (For suggestions

on foliage, see "Selecting Your Foliage," page 28.) To make

the design viewable from either side, bouquets

of foliage are bound to the wreath base in a spiral pattern,

thus completely concealing the wire form.

To give the wreath a double-sided, boxlike border, two

wooden frames are glued back to back,

with the wreath suspended inside.

Materials

- *125 fresh foliage sprigs, each about 3in (7.5cm) long*
- *Two 10 x 10 x 1³⁄₈in (25.5 x 25.5 x 3.5cm) wooden box-style picture frames*
- *18-gauge florist's wire*
- *28-gauge florist's wire*
- *24-gauge brass wire*
- *Green florist's tape*
- *White acrylic craft paint*
- *Wood glue*

YOU'LL ALSO NEED:
4–5in (10.5–12.5cm)-diameter container (e.g., coffee can); light-weight pruning shears; wire cutters; staple gun; 1in (2.5cm) flat brush; and ruler.

Instructions

1. *Make wreath base.* Wind 18-gauge wire three times around container (see illustration A, facing page). Slide wire circle off container, clip wire from spool, and bind entire circle with florist's tape.

2. *Assemble bouquets.* Gather five or six foliage sprigs into bouquet and bind lower ½in (12mm) of stems with florist's tape. Repeat to make twenty-five to thirty bouquets.

3. *Bind bouquets to base.* Lay one bouquet against wreath base, then bind stem to base with 28-gauge wire. Position second bouquet on base so foliage overlaps stem of first bouquet, then bind stem to base (illustration B). Continue binding bouquets to base, concealing previous bouquet's stem with foliage of new bouquet. For a full, rounded wreath, spiral bouquets around base as you go. When you reach starting point, slip final bouquet's stem under foliage of first bouquet, bind securely, and clip wire. Examine wreath from both sides and fill in gaps as necessary.

4. *Attach wreath to frame.* Paint each frame with two coats white acrylic paint; let dry twenty minutes between coats. Cut two 7in (18cm) lengths brass wire. Loop middle of wires once around wreath at top and bottom, letting free ends of wire extend. Lay one frame face down, and center wreath inside it. Staple free wire ends to outside edge of frame, pulling wire taut so wreath is suspended (illustration C). To conceal staples, glue frames back to back with wood glue. Let dry overnight before displaying.

SELECTING FOLIAGE

This wreath requires foliage that can survive without a water source. Good choices include variegated pitt (used on the wreath here), boxwood, rose leaves, eucalyptus, miniature holly, cedar, lemon, and caspia, as these types of foliage look attractive fresh or dried. See "Keeping Fresh Foliage Hydrated," page 24, for further reference. Alternatively, use artificial foliage, or add berries, fruit, or other decorative material as desired.

Making the Wreath

designer's tip
✳ ✳ ✳ ✳ ✳ ✳ ✳

**For an interesting visual effect,
make several versions of this
wreath by mixing and matching
the foliage on each wreath,
or by lining the interior of
the frames with giftwrap.**

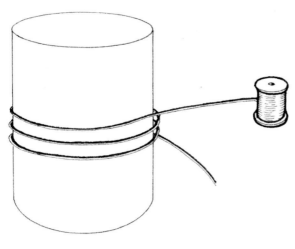

A. Wind wire around a can to shape the wreath base.

B. Bind the bouquets to the wreath base.

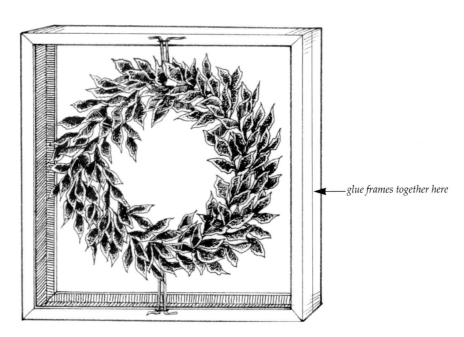

glue frames together here

C. Suspend the wreath inside a pair of wooden frames.

Ornaments

Ornaments can add a festive touch not only

to the Christmas tree, but also to the

mantel, table, windows, and doors. In this chapter,

you'll find a variety of ornaments that are evocative

of the warmth, joy, and whimsy of the season and reminiscent

of Christmases past. Old-fashioned blown-glass

ornaments, once made by hand-weaving miniature glass beads

onto thin wire strands to form stars, inspired the trio

of beaded star ornaments. You'll also find several ball ornaments:

Intricately patterned with embossed glitter, enhanced

by images of decoupage cherubs, or painted and decorated with

foil stars, these ornaments will infuse your

Christmas tree with light and beauty.

Trio of Glass Balls

A plain glass ornament can be enhanced in a variety

of ways. Here are three easy ways to decorate

glass balls: a no-glue decoupage method, a pour-in paint

technique, and a reverse-stencilling method.

The no-glue decoupage method utilizes stickers, while the

pour-in paint technique applies the paint

to the inside of the glass ball rather than to the outside.

The reverse-stencil technique lets you

block off areas of the ball with rubber bands, then adhere

glitter to the remainder of the ornament.

Materials

STICKER DECOUPAGE ORNAMENT

Yields one ornament

- *3–4in (7.5–10cm)-diameter glass ball ornament*
- *Two to three 5in (12.5cm)-square sheets composition gold leaf*
- *2½ oz (75ml) gold leaf size*
- *Brown marker*
- *Pair of 2½ x 4in (6.5 x 10cm) cherub or floral stickers*

YOU'LL ALSO NEED:

plastic drinking straw; brown kraft paper; one ¼in (6mm) and two ½in (12mm) round soft-bristled paint-brushes; manicure scissors; florist's foam brick; masking tape; wooden coffee stirrer; paper towels; spray glass cleaner; cotton ball; table knife; ruler; and mineral spirits or turpentine.

Instructions

STICKER DECOUPAGE ORNAMENT

1. *Prepare ornament for decoupage.* Remove ornament cap. Insert straw into opening, then wrap masking tape around straw and neck of ball. To free both hands during work, insert straw "handle" into foam brick as needed.

2. *Prepare stickers by clipping into individual motifs.* Make tiny clips (⅜in [9mm] deep and about ⅜in [9mm] apart) perpendicular to edge around perimeter of each cutout (see illustration A, facing page). If possible, position cuts along breaks or contours in image. If necessary, stain raw paper edges using marker.

3. *Position and affix sticker to ball.* Clean ball with glass cleaner and paper towels. Peel backing off sticker and position it on ball (illustration B). Use coffee stirrer to smooth sticker from center out, so clipped edges overlap as they conform to ball's curves. Repeat to affix second sticker to opposite side of ball.

4. *Prepare ball for gold leaf.* Cover work surface with kraft paper. Using ¼in (6mm) brush, apply size to glass ball around edges of each sticker (illustration C), then use ½in (12mm) brush to apply size to rest of ball. Let dry 5–15 minutes; clean brushes in mineral spirits. Gently place two sheets of gold leaf onto work surface. Use fingers to tear both sheets into irregular 1–2in (2.5–5cm) pieces.

5. *Apply gold leaf.* Test tack by touching tip of coffee stirrer to surface of ball; stirrer should stick and pull off as if touched to transparent tape. When size is tacky, touch fingertip to piece of leaf, lift and transfer to ball, and gently tap in place. Repeat, tearing additional leaf if necessary, until entire ball is covered (illustration D). Press dry ½in (12mm) brush gently over entire surface. Let ball dry overnight, then burnish surface by rubbing gently with cotton ball. Remove tape and straw and replace cap.

Making the Sticker Decoupage Ornament

A. To prepare the sticker, make small cuts about ⅜in (9mm) around the edges.

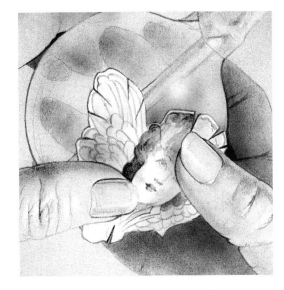

B. Overlap the clipped edges as you press the sticker to the ball.

C. Apply size to the areas surrounding the sticker.

D. When the size is tacky (5–15 minutes), apply the gold leaf using your fingertip.

Materials

POUR-IN PAINT ORNAMENT

Yields two ornaments

■ *Two 2½–3in (6.5cm–7.5cm)-
  diameter glass ball ornaments*

■ *¾in (18mm) adhesive foil star
  stickers*

■ *2oz (60ml) white acrylic craft paint*

YOU'LL ALSO NEED:

*two 3oz (90ml) disposable cups;
wooden coffee stirrer; paper towels;
spray glass cleaner; and single-hole
punch.*

POUR-IN PAINT ORNAMENT

1. *Pour paint.* To prepare cups for drying process, punch holes around rims. Remove ornament cap from one ball. Pour half of acrylic paint into ball through opening (illustration E).

2. *Distribute paint.* To distribute paint, rotate ball so paint coats entire inside surface (illustration F), then pour excess paint back into original container.

3. *Let paint dry.* To dry paint, set ball open end down into cup (illustration G). Punched holes will allow air to circulate freely. Repeat steps 1–3 to paint second ball. Let balls drain 24 hours or until inside of each is completely dry.

4. *Apply and burnish stickers.* Clean balls with glass cleaner and paper towels. Apply stars to ball surfaces at random. Burnish each sticker with coffee stirrer, pressing gently from center out to edges (illustration H). Replace ornament caps.

Making the Pour-In Paint Ornament

E. Pour acrylic paint into the ball through its opening.

F. Rotate the ball so the paint coats the inside surface.

G. Set the ball into the cup and let it drain 24 hours.

H. Apply the star stickers, then burnish them with a coffee stirrer.

REVERSE-STENCIL ORNAMENT

1. *Prepare ornament.* Remove ornament cap from one ball. Insert straw into opening, then wrap masking tape around straw and neck of ball. Clean ball with glass cleaner. To free both hands during work, insert straw "handle" into foam brick as needed.

2. *Apply "masks."* Select rubber band slightly smaller than ball diameter. Stretch rubber band around circumference of ball, then release band gently. Add two additional rubber bands parallel to first band, adjusting spacing as necessary. Brush glue over entire surface of ball, covering rubber bands (illustration I).

3. *Roll balls in glitter.* Pour embossing powder onto typing paper. Holding straw handle, roll ball in powder, manipulating paper to coat all surfaces (illustration J). Place handle in foam brick. Repeat steps 1–3 for second ball. Let balls dry 1 hour.

4. *Remove "masks."* Lift rubber bands with straight pin, clip with scissors, and pull off using tweezers (illustration K). Remove tape and straws. Replace ornament caps.

Materials

REVERSE-STENCIL ORNAMENT

Yields two ornaments

- *Two 2½–3in (6.5cm–7.5cm)-diameter glass ball ornaments*
- *1 packet (approximately 20g) gold embossing powder*
- *White high-tack craft glue*
- *¼in (6mm)-wide rubber bands in assorted sizes*

YOU'LL ALSO NEED:

½in (12mm)-wide stiff paintbrush; plastic drinking straw; florist's foam brick; masking tape; paper towels; spray glass cleaner; sheet of typing paper; tweezers; and scissors.

Making the Reverse-Stencil Ornament

I. Stretch the rubber bands around the ball, then brush glue over the entire surface.

J. Roll the ball in the embossing powder, moving the paper to coat the entire surface.

K. Clip the rubber bands with scissors, then peel them off with tweezers.

Embossed
Tree Ornaments

These charming fruit and vegetable

ornaments feature a soft, satiny, three-dimensional

look. To achieve this effect, you'll need

a sheet of aluminum, which is thin, lightweight, and

easily cut into shapes with scissors.

The shapes are embossed from behind using a pencil

eraser and colored with glass paint,

resulting in ornaments that look like handblown glass.

Materials

Yields three ornaments

- *36-gauge aluminum embossing foil*
- *16-gauge aluminum armature spool wire*
- *24-gauge silver spool wire*
- *Transparent glass paints, ⅔oz (20ml) each in light red, light green, violet, yellow, and colorless extender*
- *Microfine glitter in silver, pale gold, and green*
- *Fine elastic cord*
- *Matte acrylic spray sealer*
- *Craft glue*

YOU'LL ALSO NEED:

fruit and vegetable patterns (see page 180); #2 graphite pencil with blunt point and add-on eraser cap; ¹⁄₁₆in (1.5mm)-thick foam pad; denatured alcohol; #10 sabeline brush; sturdy utility scissors; manicure scissors; ¾oz (22.5ml) transparent glass paint thinner; wire cutters or pliers with wire-cutting ability; steel nail file; orange stick; circle drafting template; access to photocopier; unopened small soup can; craft sticks; baby food jars; paper towels; cotton swabs; wooden slats; masking tape; sheet of typing paper; and stainless steel teaspoon.

Instructions

MAKING THE ORNAMENTS

1. *Transfer patterns to foil.* Photocopy patterns (see page 180), then rough-cut ½in (12mm) beyond pattern outlines all around. Tape patterns, right side up, to embossing foil, then slip foam pad underneath foil. Trace all circles and arcs with blunt pencil, using heavy pressure to indent foil as follows: For tomato, align tin can on pattern and trace around can rim, skipping over stem area. For pea pods (make two), use circle template to draw various-sized peas. For grapes, use circle template to draw whole grape at center and arcs clustered around it (see illustration A, facing page). Rest foil on hard surface and lightly trace grape leaf and all remaining lines, including dashed stem lines. Untape and remove patterns. Slip pad back under foil and deepen all freehand lines except stem lines by retracing.

2. *Emboss foil from wrong side.* Turn foil face down on foam pad. Rub areas within traced lines in circular motion using eraser end of pencil, pressing down and hollowing out foil in back to create raised, gently rounded surface on right side (illustration B). Work several rounds in succession to stretch and shape foil gradually, instead of trying to achieve full depth in one particular area at once. For tomato, use pointed end of orange stick to push out tips on stem, then run back of teaspoon against broad lower bowl to smooth out bumps and create full, swelling shape. For pea pods, sweep eraser down edges to create gentle rippling, then emboss individual peas. Emboss grapes so those at middle protrude more than those at sides. When done, turn each piece right side up on hard surface and run pencil over any lines that have lost clarity.

3. *Cut out embossed ornaments.* Rough-cut each ornament ¼in (6mm) beyond outlines using utility scissors. Use manicure scissors to trim off allowance just outside pencil lines and along stem lines (illustration C). Cut into deep Vs first, trim out excess, then cut rounded parts. Cut tips of pea pods so they are blunt and rounded instead of sharp. Smooth cut edges by running steel nail file against edges at 45° angle from both sides. Gently push out and swell center of grapes and tomato using thumb.

4. *Add stems to grape leaf and pea pods.* Cut 14in (35cm) length from armature wire using wire cutters or pliers. Set armature wire against wrong side of grape leaf so ½in (12mm) extends into leaf area (illustration D, page 43). Lay 24-gauge wire alongside armature stem wire so end is even with bottom of leaf stem. Using pliers, roll foil stem

Tracing and Embossing the Ornaments

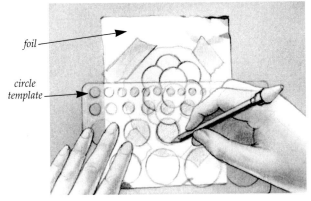

foil —

circle
template —

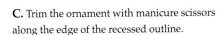

A. Transfer the fruit or vegetable design to aluminum. Use a circle template to make perfect circles and arcs.

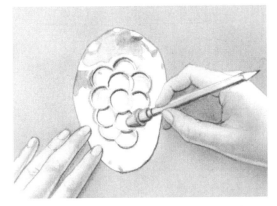

B. Emboss the design from the back using a pencil with an add-on eraser cap.

C. Trim the ornament with manicure scissors along the edge of the recessed outline.

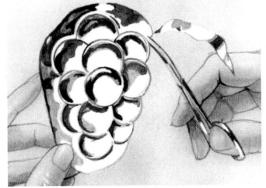

bottom of leaf around both wires from both sides, then crimp around the wires (illustration E). Wind 24-gauge wire down around entire leaf stem in tight spiral, clip off end, and crimp securely (illustration F). Repeat to add 8in (20.5cm) stem to each grape leaf and pea pod.

PAINTING THE ORNAMENTS

1. *Prepare ornaments for painting.* Work in well-ventilated room and cover work surface with newsprint. Clean each ornament with denatured alcohol and paper towel. Use cotton swab dipped in alcohol to clean crevices. To prevent painted ornaments from adhering to newsprint, lay two wooden slats parallel to each other on newsprint, then lay ornaments across them, spanning space in between (illustration G).

2. *Apply glass paints.* Mix colors, as noted in "Working with Glass Paint on Foil," below. Using sabeline brush, apply thin coat of paint to each outlined section of ornaments. Use craft sticks and baby food jars for mixing. Clean brush with thinner between colors. Apply paint as follows: a) light green paint to tomato stem and grape leaf; b) 2 parts yellow + 1 part light green to outer area of pea pods (do not paint peas); c) light red to tomato; d) 1 part violet + 2 parts extender to grapes. Let ornaments dry overnight. Holding spray sealer can 18in (46cm) above work surface, apply matte spray to ornaments; let dry 1 hour. Paint individual peas using yellow paint.

FINISHING THE ORNAMENTS

1. *Glue glitter to stems.* Working over sheet of typing paper, brush extender onto tomato stem, then sprinkle with green microfine glitter. Shake off excess glitter onto paper and funnel back into container. For peas, twist wire stems together in free-form curlicue or twist around pencil. Brush stems with extender and sprinkle with silver microfine glitter as just described. For grape leaf, curl portion of stem nearest leaf into ½in (12mm) loop and wind remaining portion around pencil to form tight spiral (illustration H). Brush entire stem with colorless extender and sprinkle with pale gold microfine glitter as above. Let dry ½ hour. Use dry brush to whisk off excess glitter from ornaments.

2. *Add hanging loops.* Using glue, affix loop of grape leaf stem to top back of grape cluster. Let dry overnight. Cut three 8in (20.5cm) lengths of elastic cord and knot ends of each together. Glue one to back of tomato for hanger. Let dry overnight. Loop remaining two around pea and grape stems.

WORKING WITH GLASS PAINT ON FOIL

Glass paint is frequently mixed with a colorless extender, essentially a clear lacquer, which can be used to thin out the colors and to add shading effects. Because glass paints are meant to be applied to glass, held against light, and seen through, the darker colors are more saturated. Since you will be applying the paints directly to metal, which is opaque, you will need a large amount of extender to lighten darker colors, such as violet, blue, and green. Apply the paint in a very thin coat to allow some of the aluminum's silvery shine to show through.

Finishing the Ornaments

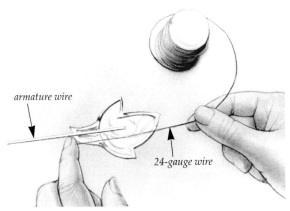

D. To create a stem for the grape leaf, lay armature wire and 24-gauge wire side by side.

armature wire

24-gauge wire

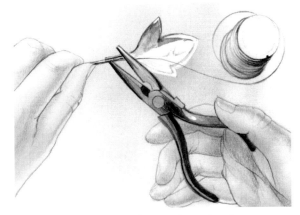

E. Wrap the foil around both wires, then crimp down on them using the pliers.

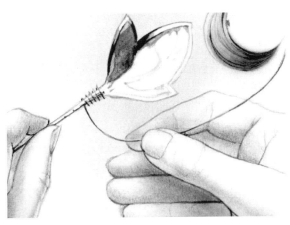

F. Use the 24-gauge wire to bind the entire length of the stem.

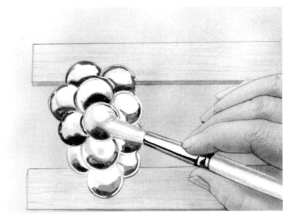

G. To prevent the ornaments from adhering to the newsprint during painting, lay them across two slats of wood.

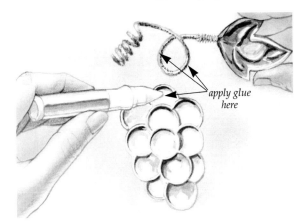

apply glue here

H. Coat the wire stem with fine glitter, then glue it to the back of the ornament.

Glitter Balls

Here's a fun way to make beautiful

Christmas ornaments with speed: "Glue" microfine

glitter or embossing powder to any color

glass ball ornament using transparent double-sided tape.

Wrap the tape around the circumference

of the ball, then roll the ball in glitter or embossing

powder to adhere it to the tape.

To add second or third colors, apply new tape

strips, then repeat the process.

Materials

Yields two ornaments

- *Two 2½–3in (6.5–7.5cm)-diameter glass ball ornaments, one red, one gold*
- *Transparent double-sided tape, ¼in (6mm) wide*
- *1 packet (approximately 20 grams) each microfine glitter or embossing powder in gold, blue, and red*

YOU'LL ALSO NEED:

gridded self-healing cutting mat; craft knife; steel-edged ruler; paper towels; spray glass cleaner; several sheets of typing paper; ¼in (6mm)-wide stiff paintbrush; and scissors.

OTHER ITEMS, IF NECESSARY:

cotton swabs and denatured alcohol (for removing excess adhesive).

Instructions

1. *Prepare ornament.* Remove ornament cap from red ball. Clean ball with glass cleaner and paper towels.

2. *Cut and wrap tape around ball.* Lay tape on gridded mat and slice off three 8–9½in (20.5–24cm)-long sections using craft knife and ruler. Wrap one strip of tape around circumference of ball. Trim so ends butt or overlap slightly (see illustration A, facing page). Starting just inside top center of ball neck, firmly attach second piece of tape, then go around ball and back to neck on opposite side (illustration B). Trim excess and press tape into inside of neck. Repeat process for third piece of tape on other side of ball.

3. *Coat ornament.* Pour glitter or embossing powder onto typing paper. Roll ball in powder, manipulating paper to coat all taped surfaces (illustration C). Place cap back on ball. Brush excess glitter or powder from glass, if necessary. Funnel excess glitter or powder back into packet.

VARIATIONS IN DESIGN

For a variation on this ornament, cut small squares, rectangles, or other shapes of double-sided tape instead of full strips for an all-over design. You can also create a multicolor ornament. Add a few shapes at a time, then roll the ball in different colored embossing powders as you go.

Making the Glitter Balls

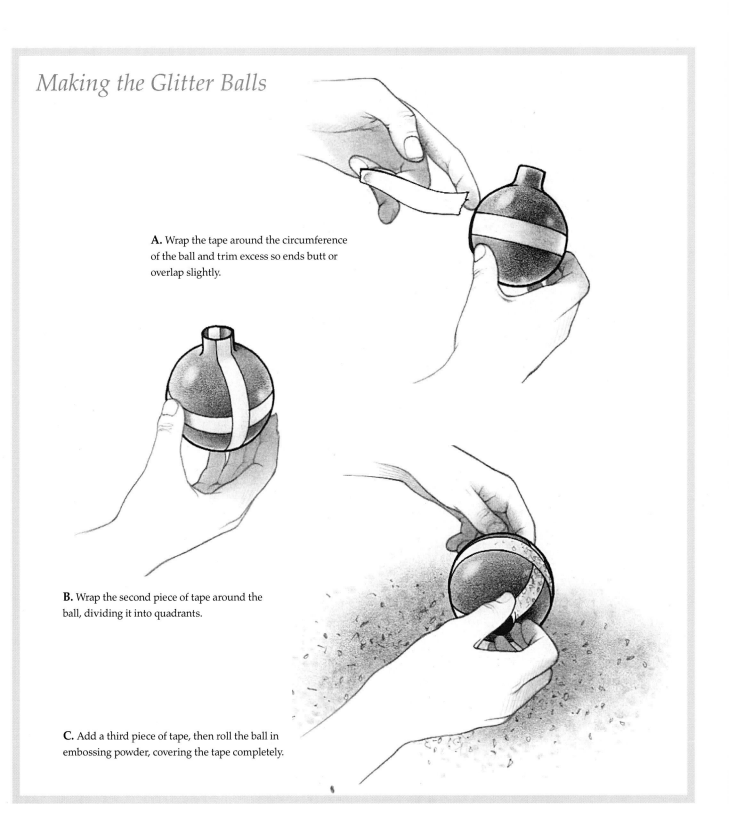

A. Wrap the tape around the circumference of the ball and trim excess so ends butt or overlap slightly.

B. Wrap the second piece of tape around the ball, dividing it into quadrants.

C. Add a third piece of tape, then roll the ball in embossing powder, covering the tape completely.

Crystal and Wire Ornaments

Because the beads are strung before the ornament

is shaped, this delicate, jewellike

design looks more complex than it actually is.

Begin by making a beaded wire circle:

wrap 24-gauge wire around a slightly heavier wire,

stringing on beads every second or third

wrap, shaping the wire into a sphere, and binding the

ends together. Repeat these steps to

make additional spheres. When you bind them together,

you can create the ornament you see here.

Materials

Yields one ornament

- 50 6mm round faceted glass beads, assorted colors as desired
- 20-gauge silver spool wire
- 24-gauge silver spool wire
- 28-gauge silver spool wire

YOU'LL ALSO NEED:

needle-nose pliers; wire cutters; soda can; and flannel cloth.

designer's tip
* * * * * * *

For a variation on this ornament, use beads in a single color, in two or three shades of a single color, or in two complementary colors. A multicolored ornament in jewel tones—red, blue, amber, and green—would also be attractive.

Instructions.

1. *Sort beads.* Lay beads on flannel cloth and line them in desired order. Repeat until all beads are set out.

2. *String beads.* Cut 10in (25.4cm) of 20-gauge wire. Unwind some 24-gauge wire from spool, but do not cut. Holding the ends of 20- and 24-gauge wires together, twist 24-gauge wire around 20-gauge wire two or three times, to form spiral about ½in (12mm) long. Pull 24-gauge wire aside, then slip first bead from lineup onto 20-gauge wire, and slide it down to spiraled section. Twist 24-gauge wire around 20-gauge wire two or three times, locking bead in place. Slip on second bead from lineup and twist wire to trap bead. Repeat process, continuing until all beads are strung or you reach end of 20-gauge wire; to end off, spiral 24-gauge wire around 20-gauge wire for ½in (12mm) and clip wire from spool (see illustration A, facing page). Wrap 20-gauge wire five or six complete revolutions around soda can, add 1in (2.5cm), (for binding sphere later on) and clip with wire cutters.

3. *Shape first round of wire sphere.* Cut two 6in (15cm) lengths of 28-gauge wire; set one length aside. To establish circumference, wrap beaded wire once around can. Hold intersection securely, and slip wire circle off can. To anchor intersection, pinch ends together, then bind once or twice with one length of 28-gauge wire; do not trim 28-gauge wire end (illustration B).

4. *Shape successive rounds of sphere.* Slide one hand 8–10in (20.5–25cm) down beaded wire and draw up into same-size circle formed in step 3. Bind together at established intersection, using extra 20-gauge wire; use reserved 28-gauge wire to bind intersection at opposite pole. If a bead interferes with intersection, adjust spiraled wire position and manipulate bead out of way. Bend second circle slightly so it runs alongside first circle, forming segment on imaginary sphere. Continue shaping and lashing beaded wire circles, segment by segment, until sphere is complete (illustration C). To end off, bind securely, then clip and crimp end (illustration D).

Making the Crystal and Wire Ornaments

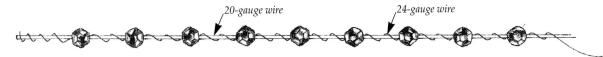

20-gauge wire   24-gauge wire

A. Combine thin spiraling wire and glass beads on a single strand.

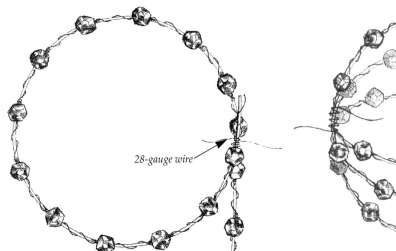

28-gauge wire

B. Shape and bind the beaded strand into a circle.

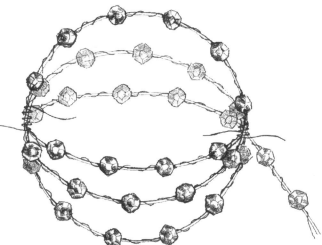

C. Form additional circles to create a beaded sphere.

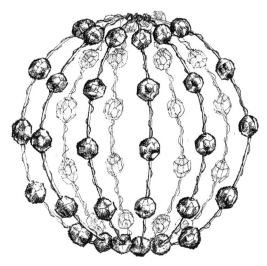

D. To end off, bind securely, then clip and crimp end.

Beaded Star Ornaments

Silvery old-fashioned beaded star

ornaments add glamour to any Christmas tree.

The base for each of the ornaments

shown here is a center core that can be made from

either a cork bob (available at fishing

supply or tackle shops) or a filigree bead, through

which three wires are inserted to create

six arms. Each ornament is finished by threading

a variety of beads on each arm. The

ornaments shown in the photograph at left are

Graduated Bead Star (upper left),

Teardrop Star (center), and Circle Star (lower left).

Materials

TEARDROP STAR

- ¾in (18mm)-diameter cork fishing bob
- 6 silver 1in (2.5cm) teardrop beads
- 6 gold 5mm x 9mm faceted flat beads
- 6 silver 10mm-diameter beads
- 6 silver 6mm-diameter beads
- 6 silver 4mm-diameter beads
- 20-gauge silver wire
- Pale gold microfine glitter
- High-tack glue
- Sand-colored wood putty
- 1in (2.5cm) brad

GRADUATED BEAD STAR

- ¾in (18mm)-diameter silver filigree bead
- 6 silver 12mm-diameter beads
- 6 silver 10mm-diameter beads
- 6 silver 6mm-diameter beads
- 6 silver 4mm-diameter beads
- 20-gauge silver wire
- Silver microfine glitter
- High-tack craft glue

YOU'LL ALSO NEED:
needle-nose pliers with wire cutters; round-nose pliers; ruler; pencil; small, stiff brush; ornament hanger; waxed paper; and sheet of scrap paper.

Instructions

TEARDROP STAR

1. *Make six-spoke base.* Fill precut holes in cork with wood putty using fingertip. Draw bisecting line around cork, then mark six dots evenly spaced on line (see illustration A, p. 56). To "drill" channels for wire, set brad point on each dot in turn and push in toward center of cork. Cut three 7in (18cm) lengths of wire. Push end of one wire into one channel so it emerges on opposite side. Insert second and third wires through remaining channels; adjust wires so ends are equal in length (illustration B).

2. *Coat cork with glitter.* Fold scrap paper in half, then open flat. Holding base by wires over paper, brush cork surface with glue. Sprinkle glitter over cork, rotating it to coat entire surface. Lay on waxed paper and let dry one hour. Funnel excess glitter back into container.

3. *String beads on spokes.* Working one spoke at a time, string beads in following order: one gold flat, one silver 6mm, one silver teardrop, one silver 10mm, and one silver 4mm (illustration C). Slide beads toward cork. To eliminate slack, bend wire at 45° angle using pliers, and clip ¼in (6mm) from bend (illustration D). Grip short end with round-nose pliers and bend in opposite direction, forming small loop (illustration E). Repeat to string and finish remaining spokes (illustration F). Thread ornament hanger through loop end of one spoke.

GRADUATED BEAD STAR

1. *Make six-spoke base.* Cut three 6in (15cm) lengths of wire. Push one wire into filigree bead so it emerges on opposite side. Insert second and third wires into bead on same plane, curving wire slightly to facilitate pass-through. Reposition wires if necessary to make six spokes equidistant from each other, adjust wires so ends are equal in length (illustration G, page 57).

2. *String beads on spokes.* Working one spoke at a time, string silver beads in following order: 12mm, 10mm, 6mm, 4mm (illustration G). End off as for Teardrop Star, step 3 (illustrations D and E, page 56). Repeat to string and finish remaining spokes (illustration H).

CIRCLE STAR

1. *Make six-spoke base.* Cut three 7in (18cm) lengths of 20-gauge wire. Push one wire into filigree bead so it emerges on opposite side. Insert second and third wires into bead on same plane, curving wire slightly to facilitate pass-through. Reposition wires if necessary to make six spokes equidistant from each other, adjust wires so ends are equal in length (illustration I).

2. *String beads on spokes.* Working one spoke at a time, string beads in following order: one 8mm bugle, one silver 6mm, one 8mm bugle, one bronze 3mm, one gold flat, one silver 4mm, one pink oval, one silver 4mm, one silver oval, and one silver 4mm (illustration I). End off as for Teardrop star, Step 3 (illustrations D and E). Repeat to string and finish remaining spokes (illustration J).

3. *Join and string circle of beads.* Cut one 11in (28cm) length of 28-gauge wire. Bend wire 1in (2.5cm) from end, then wrap once around first spoke and lodge between 8mm bugle bead and bronze 3mm bead. String on silver oval bead, silver 12mm bead, and silver oval bead (illustration K). Slide beads to spoke, bend wire at end bead, and wrap around adjacent spoke between 8mm bugle bead and bronze 3mm bead. Continue stringing between remaining sections in same way to create bead circle. To end off, twist wire ends together for ¼in (6mm) and clip close to spoke.

Materials
CIRCLE STAR
- *8mm-diameter gold filigree bead*
- *18 silver mirrored 7mm x 5mm faceted oval beads*
- *6 pink mirrored 9mm x 8mm faceted oval beads*
- *6 gold 5mm x 9mm faceted flat beads*
- *12 purple 8mm bugle beads*
- *6 bronze 3mm faceted beads*
- *6 silver 12mm-diameter beads*
- *6 silver 6mm-diameter beads*
- *18 silver 4mm-diameter beads*
- *20-gauge silver wire*
- *28-gauge silver wire*

WORKING WITH CORK BOBS AND FILIGREE BEADS

If you use a cork, insert the wires into the bob before applying glue and glitter. If you apply glitter first, it will rub off as you try to insert the wires. If you have trouble getting the second and third wires inserted past the first wire in the cork or the filigree bead, curve the ends of the last two wires slightly and their ends will bypass whatever wires are already present.

Making the Bead Ornaments' Base

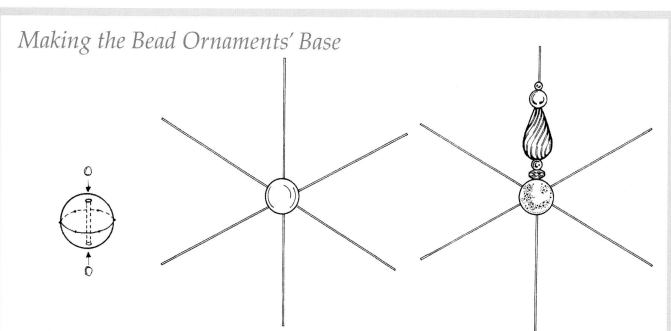

A. Plug the holes of a cork bob and mark six equidistant dots around the middle.

B. Pass three wires through the cork bob to make six spokes. Coat the cork with glitter.

C. String beads onto one wire in the sequences described.

Constructing the Teardrop Star

← *pliers*

wire loop →

D. To finish, bend the excess wire at a right angle and clip ¼in (6mm) from the top bead.

E. Use round-nose pliers to shape the end into a small loop.

F. String the remaining spokes to match, then add an ornament hanger.

Constructing the Graduated Bead Star

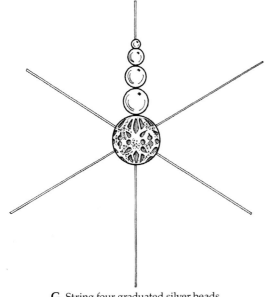

G. String four graduated silver beads onto one spoke in descending order.

H. String the remaining spokes to match, ending each one in a small loop.

Constructing the Circle Star

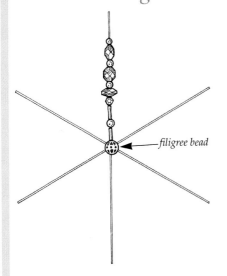

filigree bead

I. String matching spokes with beads as shown, ending each one in a small loop (see illustrations D and E).

J. To add a circle, join a new wire to one spoke and string on three beads.

K. Join the circle wire to the adjacent spoke, then string on three new beads. Repeat to make full circle.

 *Ornaments*

Moravian Glitter Stars

These striking holiday stars are fast and easy to make.

All you do is glue three sets of chipboard

triangles together into a perfect three-dimensional, twelve-

pointed star. Using the instructions, you

can make a large star, which measures 11in (28cm) high,

or a smaller star measuring 5½in (14cm) high.

Covered with glitter, several different-size stars can be

grouped to form a centerpiece, a large star

can be used as a tree topper, or a bunch of smaller ones

can be hung as ornaments.

Materials

■ *Gold microfine glitter*
■ *Gold acrylic craft paint*
■ *9 x 13in (23 x 33cm) piece two-ply chipboard*
■ *Six 18in (46cm) florist's stems*
■ *1in (2.5cm)-wide masking tape*
■ *High-tack craft glue*
■ *Cyanoacrylic glue*
■ *White craft glue*
■ *Button thread*
■ *Spray fixative*

YOU'LL ALSO NEED:

patterns (see page 180); craft knife; self-healing cutting mat; steel ruler; scissors; wire cutters; tweezers; 1in (2.5cm) flat soft-bristled brush; pencil; sheet of white copier paper; newspaper; awl; and hanging cord.

designer's tip
✳ ✳ ✳ ✳ ✳ ✳ ✳

For a faceted effect, coat one side of each triangle with gold and the other side with silver. To create a new color of glitter, combine two colors. You can make pale lavender glitter, for example, by mixing purple and silver glitter.

Instructions

1. *Cut out twelve star points.* Using pencil and steel ruler, trace one or two patterns (see page 180) on two-ply chipboard. Lay chipboard on cutting mat. Using craft knife and steel ruler, cut on marked lines to make twelve star points. For use as tree ornament, use awl to pierce hole in tip of one point.

2. *Join star points to florist's stems.* Cut 5in (12.7cm) strip of masking tape for each small star, 9in (23cm) strip for large star. Lay tape flat, sticky side up. Line up base of four star points along tape, ½in (12mm) in from long edge; trim excess tape at each end (see illustration A, facing page). Using wire cutters, cut 6in (15cm) florist's stem for each small star, 10in (25.5cm) stem for large star. Lay stem on tape, butting it against short edge of points and allowing 1 in (2.5cm) to extend at each end. Use small piece of chipboard shaped into spatula to apply high-tack glue along length of stem. Fold tape up onto points, trapping stem inside. Use craft knife to trim out excess tape between points. Repeat process to make three four-point stems per star.

3. *Join stems to make star.* Bend stem to form simple star with square opening in middle; twist and overlap wire ends to secure (illustration B). Bend second stem in same way, shape it around first star, and twist wire ends together (illustration C). Repeat process to join third stem around first two; stagger twisted joins to avoid excess bulk at any one bend (illustration D). Tape over wire ends to conceal. Tie button thread around wobbly joins (where stars intersect) to stabilize them. Seal all joins with cyanoacrylic glue. Let dry overnight.

4. *Paint star and glue on glitter.* Protect work surface with newspaper. Using flat soft-bristled brush, apply gold paint to entire star surface, including edges. Let dry twenty minutes. Clean brush. Brush white craft glue over entire star surface. Hold star with tweezers over sheet of white copier paper and sprinkle with glitter, turning star until all surfaces are covered. When done, crease paper to funnel excess glitter back into container. Repeat process to paint and glue glitter to each star, cleaning brush in between painting and gluing steps as necessary. Let dry one hour. To discourage glitter from shedding, apply spray fixative following manufacturer's instructions and working in a well-ventilated place. To use hanging hole, poke glitter from hole with pin and thread with nylon or decorative cord.

Making a Three Dimensional Star

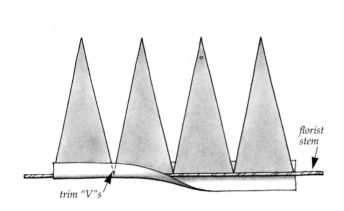

A. Tape and glue four star points to a florist's stem.

trim "V"s

florist stem

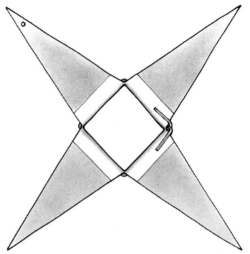

B. Bend the stem to make a flat star.

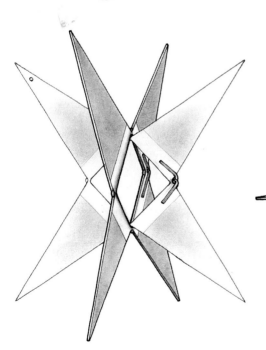

C. Bend a second stem around the first star.

D. Add a third stem for twelve points total.

Glitter Fruit

Using an assortment of plastic fruit,

all-purpose craft glue, and several shades of glitter,

you can create decorative iridescent

fruit for every corner of your home. The secret lies

in mixing contrasting colors of glitter, either

on the fruit itself to create highlights or "sun-ripened"

spots, or on the leaves to create shading effects.

Here you'll find instructions for making glitter-covered

pears, grapes, and apricots, but this project

can be adapted for use with any artificial fruit, vegetable,

or other decorative object.

Materials

- *Artificial fruit with leaves*
- *Microfine glitter in fruit and foliage colors: silver, gold, violet, bronze, willow green, moss green, celadon green, and lilac*
- *Yellow-green metallic glitter*
- *White craft glue*

YOU'LL ALSO NEED:

1in (2.5cm) foam brush; plastic palette; waxed paper; clean scrap paper (one sheet per glitter color); clothesline with clothespins and/or florist's foam bricks.

designer's tip
✳ ✳ ✳ ✳ ✳ ✳ ✳

For contrast within a fruit cluster, select colors that are opposite each other on the color wheel such as red and green or yellow and purple. To create a rich accent for a yellow-green pear, for instance, make a leaf with violet glitter.

Instructions

These instructions can be easily adapted for similar fruits.

SMALL PEARS

1. *Apply glue to pear.* Squeeze white craft glue into plastic palette. Hold one small plastic pear apart from leaves or other fruit. Using foam brush, apply glue to surface, rotating pear for full coverage (see illustration A, facing page).

2. *Apply glitter to pear.* Hold pear over sheet of clean scrap paper. Sprinkle gold glitter onto wet glue, rotating pear for full coverage (illustration B). Shake or tap gently to shed excess glitter onto paper; do not touch glittered surface. Clip cluster by stem to clothesline or stand upright in florist's foam brick; let dry one hour undisturbed. Repeat steps 1 and 2 to coat remaining fruit or other small pears in cluster. Crease paper to funnel excess glitter back into container as needed.

3. *Add highlights.* Squeeze white craft glue directly from nozzle onto pear in irregular pattern (illustration C). If glue forms ridge, blot excess with foam brush until glue lies flat. Hold pear over clean scrap paper, then sprinkle violet glitter onto wet glue and tap off excess. Repeat gluing and sprinkling process to add bronze glitter highlights. Use fresh scrap paper for each new glitter color, and funnel excess glitter back into container when done. Repeat process to highlight remaining pears. Let dry one hour as in step 2.

4. *Add glitter to leaves.* Hold one leaf apart from cluster, lay face up and flat on waxed paper, and apply glue to surface using brush. Hold leaf over scrap paper, sprinkle moss green glitter onto wet glue, and tap off excess. Repeat to apply glitter to front of as many leaves as possible while holding them apart from each other. Let dry one hour, as in step 2. Repeat process as needed to cover all leaf fronts. When dry, coat leaf undersides with willow green glitter in similar manner. On some leaf undersides, create two-tone effect: Brush glue on interior area of leaf only, and coat with moss green or bronze glitter. Next, brush glue on remaining outer border, and coat with willow green glitter (illustration D).

5. *Add glitter to stems and navels.* Apply glue directly from nozzle to stems and navels; smooth and distribute with foam brush. Sprinkle bronze glitter onto wet glue, then tap off excess. Set fruit on side on waxed paper to dry, avoiding contact with freshly glued areas.

Working with Glitter

TO COVER FRUIT COMPLETELY

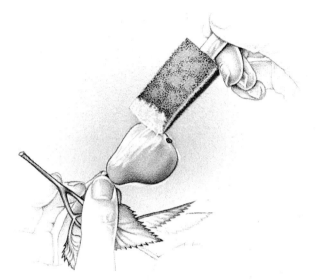

A. Use a foam brush to spread glue over the entire fruit.

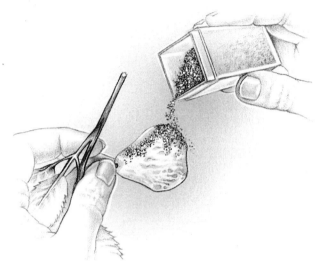

B. Sprinkle on glitter, rotating the fruit for complete coverage.

TO CREATE CONTRAST AND HIGHLIGHTS

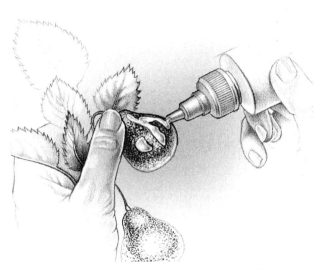

C. To add small contrasting highlights, apply glue directly from the nozzle in an irregular pattern.

D. For larger color block contrasts, apply the glue and glitter in sections.

designer's tip

✳ ✳ ✳ ✳ ✳ ✳ ✳

USES FOR GLITTER FRUIT

Use glitter fruit to decorate
garlands, wreaths, candlesticks,
place settings, mirrors, sconces,
banisters, doorknobs, chairbacks,
or curtain finials.

Use glitter fruit as package
decorations, hostess gifts, napkin
rings, mistletoe, guest-room
accents, Christmas tree
ornaments, or party favors.

Arrange glitter fruit in a glass
vase or cornucopia or within
a floral centerpiece. Scatter them
across a sideboard, string them
along a mantel, hang them from
a chandelier, cluster them in a
large glass bowl, mount them on
the corner of a picture frame, or
hang them from a door knocker.

LARGE PEAR

1. *Create glitter shading.* Squeeze white craft glue into plastic palette. Identify shaded or well-ripened areas on plastic pear, then use foam brush to apply glue to these areas only. Hold pear over sheet of scrap paper. Sprinkle yellow-green glitter onto wet glue, rotating pear as needed. Shake or tap gently to shed excess glitter onto paper, but do not touch glittered surface. Proceed to step 2 immediately to prevent glue from drying

2. *Apply glitter to remainder of pear.* Hold pear by stem. Using foam brush, apply glue to remainder of pear surface, working around glitter already in place. Hold pear over new sheet of scrap paper, sprinkle gold glitter onto wet glue, and tap off excess. Clip pear by stem to clothesline or stand upright in florist's foam brick; let dry one hour. Crease scrap paper to funnel excess glitter back into containers.

3. *Add glitter to leaves.* Follow Small Pears, step 4, but coat fronts and undersides of leaves with moss green.

4. *Add glitter to stem and navel.* Follow Small Pears, step 5.

GRAPES

1. *Apply glue and glitter to grapes.* Follow Small Pears, step 1, taking care to prevent grapes from touching each other. To coat grapes with violet glitter, follow Small Pears, steps 1 and 2, using violet glitter. To coat remaining grapes in cluster with lilac glitter, repeat steps 1 and 2. To add highlights follow Small Pears, step 3, using celadon green glitter.

2. *Add glitter to leaves and stems.* Follow Small Pears, step 4. Coat front of leaves with moss green or willow green glitter. Coat underside with willow green or silver glitter. To add glitter to stems and tendrils, follow Small Pears, step 5.

APRICOTS

1. *Create highlights.* Squeeze white craft glue into plastic palette. Identify unripe (white, yellow, or green) areas on plastic apricot, then use foam brush to apply glue to these areas. If fruit doesn't have markings, brush glue around base or stem. Hold apricot over sheet of scrap paper. Sprinkle gold glitter onto some areas of wet glue, then shake off excess. Move to clean sheet of scrap paper, and sprinkle willow green glitter over remaining wet areas, causing gold and green glitters to blend. Shake or tap gently to shed excess glitter onto paper, but do not touch glittered surface.

2. *Apply glitter to remainder of apricot.* Follow Large Pear, step 2, but use bronze glitter instead of gold.

3. *Add glitter to leaves.* Follow Small Pear, step 4. Coat front and underside of larger leaves with moss green glitter. Coat smaller leaves with willow green glitter.

4. *Add glitter to stems and navels.* Follow Small Pears, step 5.

designer's tip
✳ ✳ ✳ ✳ ✳ ✳ ✳
When shopping for plastic fruit, you may find pieces already joined in clusters or available for individual purchase. If you use fruit in clusters, separate them into individual pieces. Coat the fruit and leaves separately, as this is a more effective method. Then twine the fruit and leaf stems together, and coat the

ALL ABOUT GLITTER

Choosing the right glitter for your project depends on your taste in color, sheen, and size. Although many glitters look similar when viewed in a container, there are very real differences in the size and shape of the individual particles.

In general, there are three categories (by size) of glitter: the very smallest is called microfine, followed by regular (sometimes called fine), and last, large glitter. Microfine glitter is half the size of fine glitter and is less reflective, meaning it shows more of the color of the glitter and the object its covering. Use microfine glitter for a more sophisticated finish, since the extremely fine particles cover the surface more evenly and completely than larger grades. Regular and large glitter particles reflect light with more intensity per particle, giving the project a slightly more choppy surface. Regular glitter, the most common type of glitter found in craft stores, can be used on almost any project. Large glitter is more confetti-like in appearance, and the particles can be hexagon, star, oval, or square in shape. It is best suited for large-scale projects, such as posters, theater props, and the like.

Keepsake Silver Bird Ornament

The idea behind this heirloom-quality

Christmas ornament is fast and easy. Transform an

inexpensive Styrofoam® bird, used for

decorating wreaths into a faux silver-plated ornament

using a leafing kit. Then glue the silver-

plated bird to a wire perch to display the ornament

on a branch of a Christmas tree.

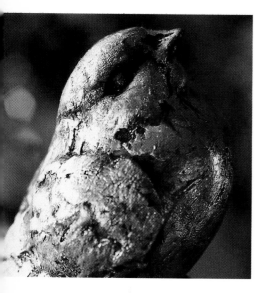

Materials

- 3in (7.5cm)-long foam bird
- Two 1in (2.5cm) long hollow silver beads (for counterweight)
- 4in (10cm) 14-gauge galvanized steel wire
- 6in (15cm) 20-gauge silver wire
- Silver leafing kit*

*Should contain sealer, base coat, adhesive, foil, and antiquing medium.

YOU'LL ALSO NEED:
round-nose pliers; needle-nose pliers; wire cutters; 1/4in (6mm) soft, flat paintbrush; small scissors; hot-glue gun; soft cloth and florist's foam brick.

Instructions

Note: Clean brush promptly in warm soapy water after each use.

1. Apply sealer and gray base coat. To make temporary handle for bird, uncoil and straighten wire feet or insert short length of 14-gauge wire into base. To free hands during work, insert feet or wire into florist's foam brick so bird stands upright. Using soft brush, apply sealer over entire bird, working from bottom up. Let dry one hour. Repeat to apply gray base coat paint (see illustration A, facing page). Let dry one hour.

2. Apply adhesive. Brush one coat adhesive onto bird; let dry until clear and tacky (up to one hour). To test for tackiness, press finger against bird; when surface is sticky like tape, adhesive is ready. Brush on second coat. When second coat of adhesive is completely clear and tacky, proceed to next step.

3. Apply silver foil. Using scissors, cut 2 x 6in (5 x 15cm) strip of foil. Wrap strip shiny side out around bird, covering as much of surface as possible. Rub strip with fingers to transfer silver film to bird (illustration B). Peel off foil. Repeat process with new foil to coat remaining blank areas; do not recoat previously foiled areas. Let some gray base coat paint show through for antiqued look. Let dry one hour.

4. Burnish and antique surface. Using soft brush, apply very light sealer coat to entire bird; let dry twenty minutes. Brush antiquing medium (or black paint) onto surface. Wrap index finger with soft cloth, then work medium into crevices and recessed areas (illustration C). Let medium dry twenty minutes. Apply final sealer coat and let dry one hour.

5. Make wire perch. Using needle-nose pliers, bend 4in (10cm) length of 14-gauge galvanized steel wire. For smooth curves, bend wire in short sections rather than all at once. Use round-nose pliers to shape open loops at each end, to match illustration D, next page. Remove temporary handle from bird. Using small scissors, carve 1in (2.5cm)-long groove approximately 1/4in (6mm) deep in bottom of bird. Test-fit hooked end of perch in groove, then hot-glue in place (illustration D).

6. Attach counterweight. Using round-nosed pliers, bend small loop in one end of 20-gauge silver wire. Thread two silver beads on wire and push beads down to loop. Cut excess wire 1/2in (12mm) beyond bead, loop this free end, and join to lower perch loop so beads dangle freely. To hang ornament, balance perch on tree branch.

Working with Silver Leaf

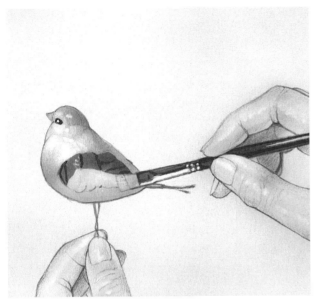

A. Apply sealer and gray base coat to a Styrofoam bird.

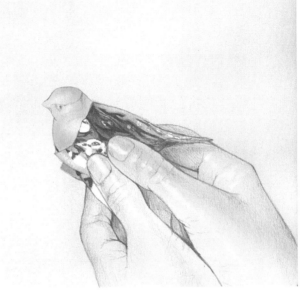

B. Apply the adhesive, then rub on the silver foil.

C. Work the antiquing medium into the crevices with a soft cloth.

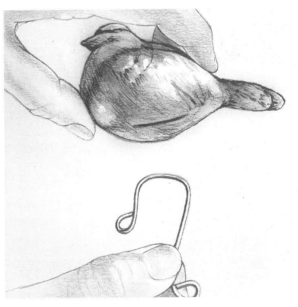

D. Make a perch from wire, then hot-glue it to a groove made in the bottom of the bird.

Mantel Decorations

Gathering with friends and family before
a crackling fire is one of the Christmas
season's finest pleasures. As the mantel is a natural
gathering place, it plays an important role in setting a joyous
mood. Adorned with handmade decorations, it
always conveys welcome. In this chapter you'll find cuffed
stockings sewn from colorful, luxurious fabrics
and an appliquéd wool stocking embellished with mistletoe leaf
and berry shapes. For decorations that sit on top
of the mantel, use a quick gilding method to give a set of
candles a handwrought antique touch, or
make a glitter village that can double as tree ornaments.

Hinged Angel Screen

This mural-like four-panel screen,

which makes an elegant mantel decoration, can

be assembled using five basic materials:

a poster, four wooden plaques, glue, decoupage

medium, and hinges. Start by cutting

the poster into four individual pieces, then

gluing them to the wooden plaques.

Seal the images with decoupage medium and

finish by hinging the panels together.

Materials

- *Angel poster at least 15in (38cm) tall x 30in (76cm) wide*
- *Four 7¼ x 13in (18.5 x 33cm) arched wood plaques with beveled edges*
- *Six 1¼in (3.2cm)-long x 1½in (3.8cm)-wide brass hinges with screws*
- *2oz (60 ml) gold metallic acrylic craft paint*
- *Gold metallic felt-tip pen*
- *Decoupage medium*

YOU'LL ALSO NEED:

1in (2.5cm)-wide foam brush; 1in (2.5cm)-wide stiff-bristled brush; craft knife; self-healing cutting mat; screwdriver or hammer; 150-grit sandpaper; 24 x 36in (61 x 91cm) sheet of newspaper (or tape smaller sheets together); paper towels; sponge; cotton balls; spray mister; and pencil.

Instructions

1. Select images. Lay four plaques edge to edge on newspaper, and trace outer edge. Remove plaques. Using craft knife and cutting mat, cut on marked line to make window in shape of plaques. Discard inner cutout portion. Lay angel poster face up on cutting mat. Lay window on top and maneuver to frame desired portion of poster (see illustration A, facing page). Trace outline lightly.

2. Cut out images. Line up wooden plaques within window, beveled edges facing down. Remove window. To cut poster, hold craft knife blade at a 45° angle and run along beveled edge of each plaque; to cut side edges, temporarily remove neighboring plaque. As you complete each cutout, set it and its plaque aside (illustration B).

3. Sand and paint panels. Using 150-grit sandpaper, lightly sand each plaque. Wipe off dust with lightly misted paper towel. Using foam brush, apply one coat gold paint to all surfaces. Let dry twenty minutes. Apply second coat, then let dry at least one hour, but preferably overnight.

4. Adhere cutouts to panels. Using stiff brush, spread decoupage medium thinly and evenly over front (beveled side) of one plaque. Position cutout on plaque and press down. Working from center out, rub cotton ball over surface in circular motion to press out air bubbles and ensure adhesion. Wipe any oozing medium from edges with damp sponge. Repeat process to adhere images to remaining plaques (illustration C). Let dry one hour. Examine. If cutout extends beyond edge, turn plaque face down on cutting mat and run craft knife along edge to trim.

5. Add finishing details. Run gold marker along white edges of cutout image. Using stiff brush, apply decoupage medium to images and onto beveled edges, brushing in different directions to simulate brush strokes of oil painting. Let dry overnight.

6. Hinge plaques together. Lay four plaques face up, side by side, in desired order. Turn second plaque face down on third plaque. Following hinge manufacturer's instructions, join left edges with two hinges placed 1½in (3.8cm) and 7½in (19cm) from bottom (illustration D). Set first plaque on second plaque, *wrong* sides together, and hinge right edges in same way. Join third and fourth plaques *wrong* sides together to complete screen (illustration E). Resulting screen will zigzag when standing up (illustration F) and fold flat for storage.

Making the Hinged Angel Screen

A. Use a newspaper window template to frame a portion of the poster.

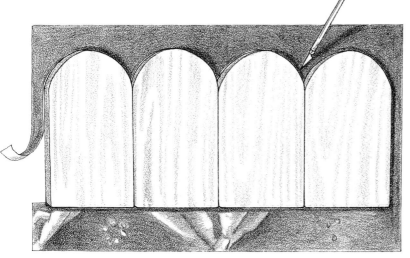

B. Use the plaques as templates to cut the poster panels.

C. Glue each poster panel to its plaque.

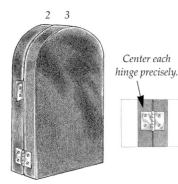

Center each hinge precisely.

D. Hinge the two middle panels right sides together.

E. Hinge each outer panel so its picture faces out.

F. Unfold the screen accordion-style to stand it upright.

Appliquéd Wool Stocking

Embellished with mistletoe leaf

and berry shapes and embroidery, this colorful

Christmas stocking combines

the homespun appeal of boiled wool with

contemporary materials

like moss fringe and pearl cotton. To make

the stocking, boil and iron the

wool, cut and sew the stocking, decorate it

with simple topstitched mistletoe

leaf and berry shapes, then embroider

the finishing touches.

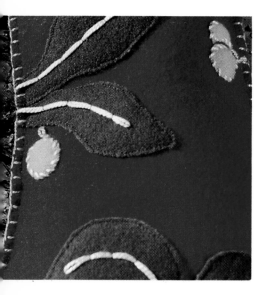

Materials

- Medium-weight wool fabric in the following sizes and colors: 22 x 32in (56 x 81.3cm) red; 11 x 22in (28 x 56cm) ivory; 11 x 15in (28 x 38cm) dark green; scraps of tan
- ½yd (46cm) 45in (1.2m)-wide cotton or muslin lining fabric
- Pearl cotton #5 in the following colors: 2 skeins gold; 1 skein yellow; 1 skein brown
- ½yd (46cm) 1in (2.5cm) yellow moss fringe
- ⅓yd (30.5cm) ½in (12mm) green upholstery braid
- 3 wooden large-hole ⅜in (9mm) beads
- Matching thread
- Scrap of batting

YOU'LL ALSO NEED:

patterns (see page 181); 8qt (8L) pot; 4qt (4L) bowl; tongs or wooden spoon; ice; dryer; iron; access to photocopier with enlarger; tracing paper; spray fixative; transparent tape; sewing machine; sharp sewing shears; embroidery or manicure scissors; tweezers; straight pins; crewel needle; old bath towel; fabric marking pen; and size 4 (3.5mm) crochet hook.

Instructions

1. *Boil and shrink wool fabrics.* Fill 4qt (4L) bowl with ice water. Fill 8qt (8L) pot halfway with water, bring to boil, and drop in ivory and tan wool fabric. Let boil 10 minutes, swishing occasionally with tongs or wooden spoon, then lift out wool and plunge into ice water for a few minutes. Remove from ice water and rinse in cold water until water runs clear. Wring fabric, roll in towel, and squeeze out excess moisture. Repeat process to shrink green and red wool fabrics individually; start with fresh water if hot bath becomes discolored. Put all fabrics in dryer and tumble dry on hot (high) setting fifteen to twenty minutes or until dry. Steam-press on wrong side. Trim fabrics to the following sizes: red—18 x 26in (46 x 66cm); ivory—9 x 18in (23 x 46cm); and green—9 x 12in (23 x 30.5cm).

2. *Make tracing patterns.* Photocopy stocking and cuff patterns onto tracing paper, enlarging 200 percent or until top edge of stocking measures 6in (15cm) across. Tape sections of photocopied stocking pattern together, if necessary, but do not cut out. Photocopy leaf and berry patterns, enlarging by 200 percent. To prevent smearing, apply spray fixative to stocking pattern pieces. Work in well ventilated work space.

3. *Pin and sew leaf appliqués.* Cut red wool in half to yield two 13 x 18in (33 x 46cm) pieces. Lay one piece right side up on flat surface, then position stocking tracing pattern on top. From green wool, cut three pieces ½in (12mm) larger all around than each leaf cluster. Slip green pieces right side up into position between pattern and red wool, adjust and/or trim them so the edges don't overlap, and secure with straight pins. Using green thread, slowly machine-stitch leaves along leaf pattern outlines through green wool, red wool, and pattern. Take your time when topstitching to prevent errors. Do not remove tracing (see illustration A, facing page).

4. *Sew stocking body with lining.* Cut two 13 x 18in (33 x 46cm) pieces from lining fabric. On flat surface, stack the following pieces: plain red wool (back piece) wrong side up; one lining right side up; one lining wrong side up; red wool from step 3 (stocking front), tracing paper face up. Pin all layers together. Using red thread and beginning and ending at dots, machine-stitch stocking outline; leave top edge open (illustration B). Transfer top edge from pattern to wool using fabric marking pen. Remove all tracing patterns. To cut out stocking, trim ¼in (6mm) beyond stitching all around and through all layers. Trim top edge along marked line. To reduce bulk, spread seam with fingers and use embroidery or manicure scissors to trim lining fabric close to seam. Using sewing shears,

Appliquéing the Stocking

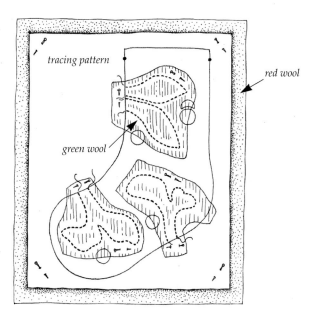

A. Sandwich the green wool between the red wool and the tracing pattern, and stitch along the leaf outlines.

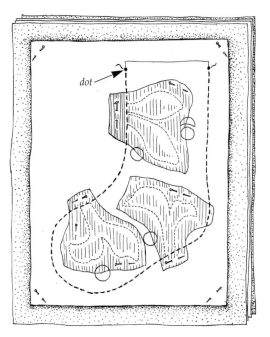

B. Stack the wool and lining fabrics together and stitch along the stocking outline from dot to dot.

trim excess green wool leaf fabric a scant 1/16in (1.5mm) beyond stitching (illustration C). Use tweezers to remove any paper or fibers that remain trapped under stitching.

5. *Attach stocking cuff.* Cut two cuffs from ivory wool and two cuffs from lining fabric. Pair each wool cuff with lining, wrong sides together. Pin one pair to front of stocking and second pair to back, wool cuff against stocking lining and edges aligned. Machine-stitch 1/4in (6mm) from stocking's top edge (illustration D). Press seams toward cuff. Sew cuffs together at sides, enclosing upholstery braid in right seam for hanging loop (illustration E). Sew fringe around inside of top edge, right sides facing (illustration F). Clip outside corners diagonally and clip into inside corners.

6. *Add berries and blanket stitching.* Fold down cuff. From tan wool, cut three berries and one half berry. Pin berries to stocking right side up (see original pattern, page 181, for placement). Using yellow pearl cotton and crewel needle, work blanket (buttonhole) or straight stitch around each berry (illustration H), taking care to sew through wool

designer's tip
✳ ✳ ✳ ✳ ✳ ✳ ✳
Boiled wool, with its dense softness, can be used for a variety of other projects including gift satchels, cosmetic bags, tea cozies, or traveling sleeves for delicate objects such as hand mirrors or perfume vials.

layer only. To make berries three-dimensional, insert small wad of batting under each one as you complete stitching. Embroider straight stitch stems to join berries to leaves (see original pattern for placement). Using gold pearl cotton and crewel needle, work blanket stitch around edge of stocking, inserting needle every third machine stitch for even placement. Using yellow pearl cotton and crewel needle, add couching (illustration I) to leaves (see original pattern for placement).

7. Add berries to cuff. Using crochet hook and gold pearl cotton, work single crochet (double crochet in Canada) around each bead until fully covered. From green wool, cut two green leaves for cuff. Using brown pearl cotton and crewel needle, tack leaves and berries to front cuff.

designer's tip
✳ ✳ ✳ ✳ ✳ ✳ ✳

Try these alternative color combinations for the Appliqué Wool Stocking:

Rust red, cerulean blue, and chrome olive green for a traditional nineteenth-century Christmas stocking.

Soft sage green, cream or chocolate-milk tan, and pink for a retro-style stocking.

Tomato red, cobalt blue or yellow-green, and chrome yellow for a stocking in the style of Murano glass.

Ivory, olive green, and chocolate brown for an autumnal stocking.

DYEING YOUR OWN WOOL

If you can't find the right color of wool fabric for your stocking, consider buying white or ivory wool and dyeing it at home. Because the fabric has to be boiled anyway, you can easily add a dye bath to the process, followed by an ice bath and a thorough washing in a washing machine to rinse out the excess dye.

Before dyeing, verify the fabric's fiber content. While 100 percent wool fabric will take color the best, you can also use a 50 percent wool/50 percent fabric blend, although you may need to experiment on test swatches to get the right color. Avoid 100 percent polyester and acrylic felts or knits, as these do not take color.

Follow the dye manufacturer's instructions carefully, although fifteen minutes in boiling hot water, with frequent stirring, is usually sufficient to both set the color and shrink the fabric to create the boiled effect. Rinse the dyed fabric in cold running water and then run it through a hot cycle on your washing machine, which will not only rinse out excess dye but soften the fabric. Tumble dry on hot as with the undyed boiled wool.

Before dyeing and washing the wool, rough-cut the dimensions as called for in the materials list, but leave at least 2-3in (5–7.6cm) around each shape to allow for shrinkage. Keep in mind, however, that fabrics shrink to different degrees. Heavier-weight wools with larger yarns will shrink more and acquire a heavier texture than thinner-weight wools with a thinner weave. If you're not sure, simply dye the entire piece and go from there.

Assembling the Stocking

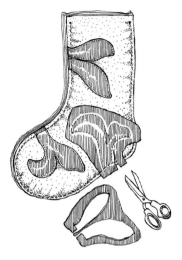  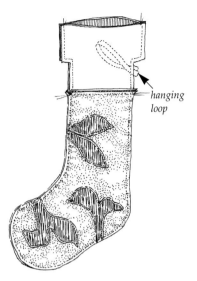

C. Remove the tracing pattern. Cut out the stocking ¼in (6mm) beyond the stitching. Trim the excess green wool close to the stitching.

D. Sew the cuff pieces to the stocking top.

E. Stitch the sides of the cuffs together, trapping the hanging loop in the seam.

hanging loop

DECORATIVE EMBROIDERY STITCHES

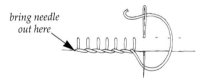

bring needle out here

H. Blanket (buttonhole) stitch: Bring the needle out on the lower line (as shown above), then insert the needle in position on the upper line, and take a straight downward stitch with the thread under the needle point. Pull up the stitch to form a loop and repeat.

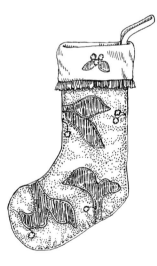 

lining

F. Sew fringe around the top edge of the stocking.

G. With the cuff folded down, add a blanket stitch edging, couching, and wooden berries (follow illustrations H and I).

I. Couching: Lay a thread along the line of the design. With another thread (contrasting or matching), tie the first thread down at even intervals with a small stitch into the fabric.

Cuffed Velvet Stocking

A soft furnishing fabric such as velvet is a beautiful

choice for a cuffed stocking, but it

unfortunately tends to droop even when lined.

There is a remedy, however. To shore

up the velvet stocking here, enclose a cord welting

in the seams. This invisible stabilizer

will firm up the edges all around while introducing

a dash of color and textural contrast.

Materials

- *½yd (46cm) 45in (1.2m)-wide velvet (for stocking)*
- *⅛yd (11.5cm) 45in (1.2m)-wide velvet (for cuff)*
- *½yd (46cm) 45in (1.2m)-wide satin or acetate*
- *1¾yd (1.6m) ¼in (6mm)-diameter cord welting*
- *4in (10cm) piece narrow ribbon or cord*
- *Matching thread*

YOU'LL ALSO NEED:

patterns (see page 186); sewing machine; iron; scissors; pins; hand-sewing needle; tracing paper; pencil; and access to photocopier with enlarger.

---

designer's tip
✳ ✳ ✳ ✳ ✳ ✳ ✳
Bright colors, such as turquoise, raspberry, moss green, and yellow, add a festive touch to holiday decorations.

Instructions

1. *Prepare patterns.* Copy and enlarge stocking and cuff pattern on page 186.

2. *Cut stocking pieces.* Fold stocking velvet in half, wrong side out, and pin stocking pattern to rectangle. Cut along marked lines to yield two mirror-image stockings. Repeat process to cut two linings from satin. Use cuff pattern in similar manner to cut two cuffs from cuff velvet.

3. *Assemble velvet cuff.* Right sides facing, stitch short edges of each velvet cuff piece together to make tube. Press seam open. Using zipper foot, machine-baste 17in (43cm) length of welting to raw edge of one cuff so "tails" hang over edge at seam as shown (see illustration A, facing page).

4. *Finish velvet cuff.* Slip one cuff tube around second cuff tube, right sides together, and align seams. Stitch all around bottom edge, over machine basting, to secure welting selvage in seam (illustration B). Turn cuff tubes right side out and press (illustration C).

5. *Attach welting to stocking.* Machine-baste remaining welting to curved raw edge of one velvet stocking (illustration D). To secure welting, stack velvet stockings, right sides together. Stitch over machine basting to secure welting in seam (illustration E). Clip curves. Do not turn.

6. *Make lining.* Stack two satin (or acetate) stockings, right sides together. Stitch curved raw edges, leaving 4in (10cm) opening on "back" seam for turning (illustration F). Turn right side out.

7. *Align cuff and lining seams.* Slip cuff inside velvet stocking, right sides together and welting at top of cuff. Align cuff seam with stocking "back" seam. Tack ends of 4in (10cm) ribbon or cord to cuff seam (illustration G).

8. *Align and attach lining.* Slip lining stocking inside velvet stocking, aligning seams and matching top raw edges. Stitch ¼in (6mm) from top raw edge all around and through all layers (illustration H). Close opening in lining. Turn stocking and lining right side out through opening in lining. Slip-stitch lining opening closed (illustration I).

Making the Velvet Stocking

A. Stitch the short edges of each cuff piece together, then machine-baste the welting to one raw edge of one cuff piece.

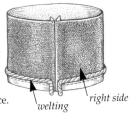

welting   *right side*

B. Slip one cuff tube around the second cuff tube, right sides together, and stitch.

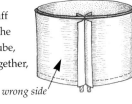

wrong side

C. Turn the cuff tubes right side out and press.

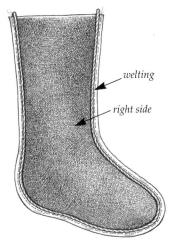

welting

right side

D. Baste the welting to the curved edge of one stocking.

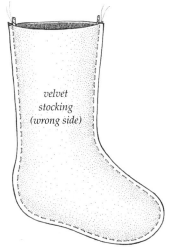

velvet stocking (wrong side)

E. Stack the velvet stockings, right sides together, then stitch.

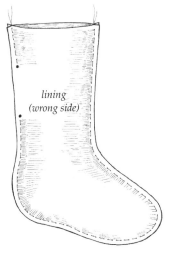

lining (wrong side)

F. Stack two lining stockings, right sides together, then stitch.

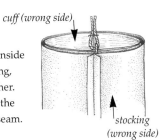

cuff (wrong side)

G. Slip the cuff inside the velvet stocking, right sides together. Tack the ends of the cord to the cuff seam.

stocking (wrong side)

stitch through all three layers   *lining*

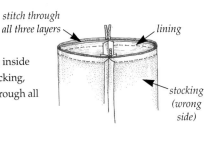

H. Slip lining inside the velvet stocking, then stitch through all layers.

stocking (wrong side)

I. Turn the stocking right side out and slip-stitch the lining opening closed.

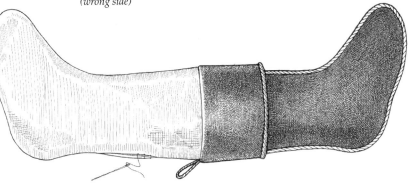

Gilded Glitter Village

Build this tiny townscape from chipboard, then

transform it into a shimmering

village using fabric paint, glitter, and beads. The main

tasks involve cutting the chipboard forms,

assembling the buildings with hot glue, painting

the buildings and covering them with

glitter, and adding the decorative details.

Materials

- *20 x 30in (51 x 76cm) piece one-ply chipboard*
- *9 x 12in (23 x 30.5cm) piece three-ply chipboard*
- *Dark gold micro glitter*
- *Pale gold glitter*
- *Silver glitter*
- *Pearlescent/antique gold fabric paint*
- *Spray adhesive*
- *Clear spray fixative*
- *White craft glue*
- *Two ½in (12.7mm) gold bells*
- *Six 4mm-diameter silver beads*
- *Three ³⁄₁₆in (4.8mm)-diameter gold crimped beads*
- *Three ³⁄₁₆in (5mm)-diameter gold filigree beads*
- *³⁄₁₆ x ³⁄₁₆ x 36in (5mm x 5mm x 1m) balsa wood stick*
- *9 x 12in (23 x 30.5cm) sheet plastic needlepoint canvas*
- *1½in (3.8cm)-diameter metal filigree finding or paper doily with filigree center*
- *Beading wire*
- *6 straight pins*

(continued on facing page)

Instructions

1. *Affix patterns to chipboard.* Prepare patterns (see page 182-184). Rough-cut each pattern ½in (12mm) beyond outlines. Working in well-ventilated work space, spray light coat of adhesive on back. Press five base patterns onto three-ply chipboard. Press remaining patterns onto one-ply chipboard with grain arrow running parallel to chipboard grain where indicated.

2. *Score and cut out patterns.* Lightly label back of each piece as you go. Lay chipboard on cutting mat. Use utility knife and ruler to cut all straight edges. Use craft knife to cut all rounded lines, including church, cathedral, and tower windows; spires; flying buttresses; bell tower; and cathedral doors. Cut clear through all solid lines and score all dashed lines. On base pieces, mark dashed lines with pencil rather than scoring them. Cut windows and doors first (do curves freehand), then cut tabs and short edges, then cut long straight lines. Peel off template paper as you go. Turn roofs face down to mark and score lines on wrong side as indicated. Sort pieces into four groups: Cottage—includes base, cottage, and roof. House—includes base, house, roof, and two shutters. Church—includes base, church, tower, roof, and spire. Cathedral—includes base, bell tower base, cathedral, door A, door B, tower A, tower B, roof, bell tower, two spires, and four flying buttresses.

3. *Add windowpanes.* Turn house, church, and cathedral face down. Cut three plastic canvas rectangles slightly larger than three largest house windows. Hot-glue canvas over window openings (see illustration A, facing page). For church and cathedral, turn canvas so squares are on diagonal, then cut rectangles large enough to cover each wall of Gothic windows (identified in illustrations F and G). Hot-glue rectangles in place. For cathedral rose window (illustration G), hot-glue metal finding within circle opening. If using cut-paper or fabric doily, spray or coat with stiffener following manufacturer's instructions, then hot-glue in place over opening from back. Glue doors A and B behind cathedral door opening to recess opening.

4. *Fold and glue main pieces.* Fold cottage, house, church, and cathedral on score lines so scoring faces out. Lap free end over tab to form box and hot-glue in place (illustration B). Fold and glue sides of three towers in same way. To add bell to church tower, pierce hole in tower top flap with needle, string bell on wire, and thread wire through hole. Adjust wire so bell is suspended inside belfry, then glue wire at top to prevent slipping. Fold each tower top flap, then tuck in and glue tabs (illustration E).

Assembling the Cottage and House

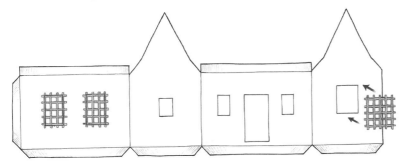

A. To make windowpanes, glue plastic canvas to the wrong side of the chipboard cutout.

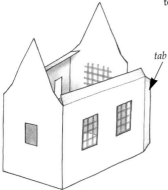

tab

B. Fold each cutout and hot-glue the side tab for a three-dimensional building.

C. Hot-glue each building to its base, pressing down the tabs with the eraser end of a pencil.

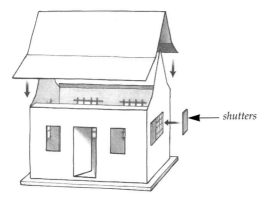

shutters

D. Hot-glue the roof to each building. Add the shutters to the house.

YOU'LL ALSO NEED:

patterns (see pages 182-184); access to photocopier with enlarger; spray adhesive; utility knife; craft knife; straight-edge steel ruler; self-healing cutting mat; hot-glue gun; newspaper; several sheets plain white paper; pencil; ½in (12mm) flat brush; ¼in (6mm) stiff stencil brush; tape; scissors; and needle.

OTHER ITEMS, IF NECESSARY:

paper stiffener (if using cut-paper doily for cathedral rose window).

designer's tip
✳ ✳ ✳ ✳ ✳ ✳ ✳

You can build on the village scene by adding trees, figures, cars, animals, or the like. Such miniatures are sold in gift, craft, and hobby shops. An assortment of miniature evergreens to offset the village's shimmering color and texture is a nice touch.

Fold and glue spires (identified in illustrations F and G) to form tall pyramids. Fold all roofs on score lines.

5. *Add base pieces and roofs.* For each building, apply hot glue generously to base within penciled outline, then immediately set structure in position (illustration C). Press inside tabs firmly against base with eraser end of pencil. Test-fit roof, apply hot glue to remaining tabs and gables, and press roof in position. Glue house shutters by end window on left side of house (illustration D). *Note:* This step concludes assembly of cottage and house. Follow Steps 6 and 7 to complete church and cathedral, then proceed for all structures to Step 8.

6. *Complete church assembly.* Referring to illustration F, hot-glue remaining church components as follows: Apply glue within tower outline of church base and to side of church, then press tower into position. Glue spire to tower. Using utility knife, cut 1¼in (3.2cm) length from balsa wood stick and glue to church base to form step at foot of door.

7. *Complete cathedral assembly.* Referring to illustration G, hot-glue remaining components as follows: Glue towers A and B to cathedral and to base as for church tower in step 6. Glue bell tower base to top of tower A. Fold bell tower, glue edges together, and add bell as for church tower, step 4, then glue bell tower to its base. Glue two spires in position. Glue flying buttresses between Gothic windows, spanning from base to upper wall. Cut three 2⅝in (6.7cm) lengths from balsa wood stick. Stack balsa wood and glue to base to form two-tier step between towers.

8. *Paint all structures.* Apply gold paint to all exposed surfaces with ½in (12mm) flat brush. Use straight, overlapping strokes for flat surfaces and circular motion to work paint into crevices and under eaves. To fill noticeable gaps, apply paint directly from dispenser tip, as if caulking. Let paint dry one hour, then apply second coat. Let dry two hours.

9. *Apply glitter to all structures.* Cover work surface with newspaper. Fold sheets of white paper in half, then unfold and set aside. Use separate sheets as needed to catch excess glitter of each color and funnel it back into containers for reuse. Using ¼in (6mm) stencil brush, apply white craft glue to all portions of each structure designated to receive pale gold glitter (as indicated below). Sprinkle glitter liberally over glued area, shake structure from side to side to distribute flakes, then tap off excess. Continue until pale gold color is applied to all structures, let dry at least ten minutes, then glue and glitter remaining areas one color at a time. Repeat process, letting dry 10 minutes in between colors, using pale gold glitter on bases, roofs, spires, house shutters, and cathedral

designer's tip
✳ ✳ ✳ ✳ ✳ ✳ ✳

The buildings that make up the gilded village also make wonderful tree ornaments. Use the patterns the same size they appear on pages 182-184, eliminate some of the more complex finishing details, and use lightweight cardboard instead of chipboard. To simplify the designs eliminate most of the windows. On walls with multiple windows, leave only one window; on walls that feature both a door and a window, keep only the door. Eliminate the steps on both churches. On the towers, skip the beads and instead substitute a round-headed pin for decoration. If desired, skip the bells in the towers as well.

To hang the ornaments, poke a hole in the roof and attach a loop of gold elastic thread or string, with a knot trapped inside. The hole in the house roofline should be centered, but move the hole forward slightly on the cathedral and the church to balance the weight of the towers.

Assembling the Church and Cathedral

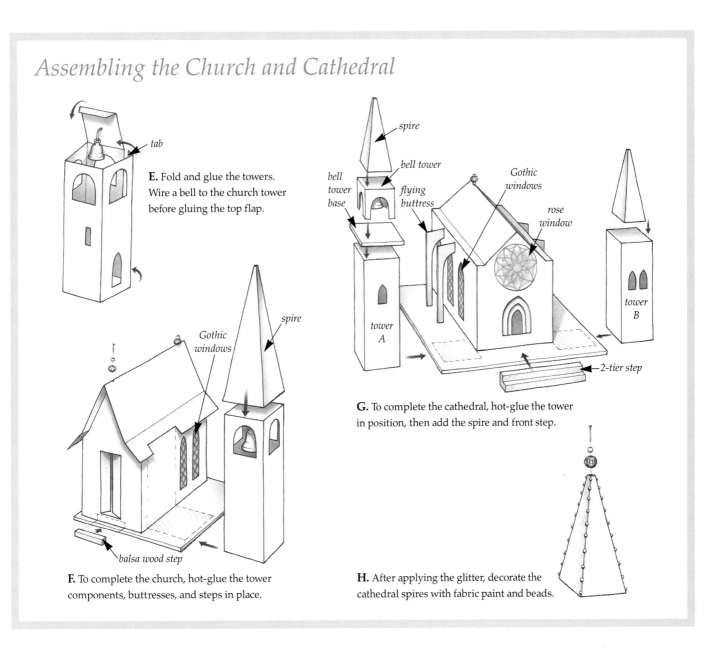

E. Fold and glue the towers. Wire a bell to the church tower before gluing the top flap.

tab

spire

bell tower

bell
tower
base

flying
buttress

Gothic
windows

rose
window

tower
A

tower
B

2-tier step

G. To complete the cathedral, hot-glue the tower in position, then add the spire and front step.

Gothic
windows

spire

balsa wood step

F. To complete the church, hot-glue the tower components, buttresses, and steps in place.

H. After applying the glitter, decorate the cathedral spires with fabric paint and beads.

buttresses; silver glitter on doors, window grilles, and rose window; and dark gold glitter on all other surfaces. Let dry overnight. To prevent flaking, spray two light coats clear spray fixative in quick succession. Let dry ten minutes.

10. *Trim spires and roofs.* Apply dots of gold fabric paint directly from dispenser tip along edges of cathedral spires. Insert straight pin through silver and gold filigree beads and glue to top of each spire (illustration H). Attach remaining silver and gold beads to each end of church roof peak and back of cathedral roof peak.

Gilded Candles

Here's a gilding project for candles

that can be completed successfully in a very short

time. Choose candles that are wrapped

in cellophane, as these already have an adhesive

surface. This way, there's no need to

use size to prepare the candles for gilding. Simply

break the gold leaf into small pieces

and press it into place on the surface of the candles.

Materials

- *Brown kraft paper (for work surface)*
- *1 book gold composition leaf (comes in book of twenty-five 5½in [14cm]-square sheets)*
- *Pillar candles, wrapped in cellophane*
- *Butter knife with blade longer than 5½in (14cm)*
- *Cotton balls*

designer's tips
✳ ✳ ✳ ✳ ✳ ✳ ✳

Composition leaf comes in many colors, including silver, copper, and aluminum. Gild candles in complementary color for an interesting display en masse. After rolling the candle in one color leaf as a backdrop, fill any remaining gaps with leaf of other colors.

It is important to work with metal leaf in a dust- and wind-free area, as it is light and easily blown about. Pets should be banned from the work area, as pet hairs readily attach themselves to adhesive surfaces.

Instructions

1. *Lay kraft paper on clean work surface.* Dampen butter knife slightly with your breath, then use knife to transfer sheet of gold composition leaf onto kraft paper (see illustration A, facing page).

2. *Unwrap candle.* Remove protective cellophane wrapper from candle, touching exposed wax as little as possible.

3. *Affix composition leaf to candle.* Break sheet of leaf into pieces using perfectly dry fingertips (illustration B). Leaf will break naturally into irregular shapes and sizes. Press pieces of leaf onto exposed areas of candle (illustration C). Alternatively, hold candle at top and bottom, lower it onto edge of leaf, then roll diagonally to adhere gold to candle

MORE PROJECT IDEAS FOR BROKEN LEAFING

The broken gold leafing technique used to decorate the candles shown here can be applied to a variety of other craft projects. Unlike the candles, however, the items listed below require size (a special glue used in leafing) in order to adhere the leaf to the surface.

Start by brushing the item with quick-dry size using a 1in (2.5cm) brush. Apply a thin, even coat, and wipe any drips before they dry. Let dry until tacky to touch (up to two hours, depending on brand of size, humidity, and temperature). Break gold leaf into pieces as with the candles, then press the pieces onto the tacky surface. Gently brush the surface with a clean 1in (2.5cm) brush to remove any loose edges, then let the object dry for at least four hours. If necessary, repeat to cover the back side of the object and let dry. Burnish the item with a cotton ball or soft cloth to remove any unattached flakes and create a soft, glowing finish. Then seal using a water-based, satin-finish sealer.

1. *Plastic fruit,* such as the pear shown at right.
2. *Plastic cherubs,* often sold as cake decorations and measuring about 3in (7.5cm) high. Gilded cherubs make great Christmas ornaments.
3. *Plain glass Christmas balls.* Paint the ball using red or silver acrylic paint, then gild over the paint. Alternatively, gild directly on the ball without an undercoat.
4. *Small decorative boxes.* Leaf the outside of the box, the inside of the box, or both.
5. *Wicker or vine baskets.* Apply the size directly to the surface, add the leaf, then burnish with a brush for a ragged leaf texture.

surface (illustration D). Repeat to affix additional sheets of leaf until surface is gilded as desired. Leave gaps ungilded for antique look or fill gaps using torn pieces as before.

4. *Burnish candle.* Rub cotton ball over candle surface to burnish leaf to shiny finish. Brush off any excess flakes of gold leaf with cotton ball.

Applying Gold Leaf to Candles

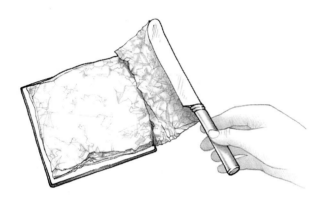

A. Lift a sheet of gold leaf using a knife blade dampened with your breath.

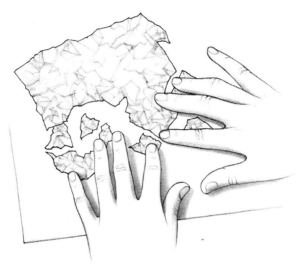

B. Break the gold leaf into pieces using perfectly dry fingertips.

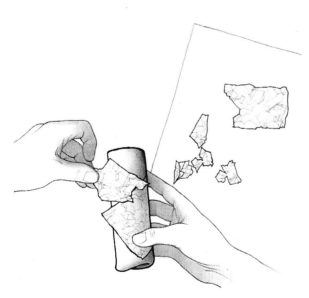

C. Press the gold leaf pieces onto the candle.

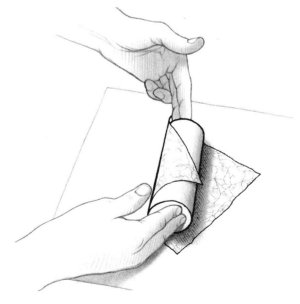

D. For more complete coverage, roll the candle diagonally across the gold leaf.

Gingerbread Birdhouses

Making a gingerbread house is usually a time-consuming

and laborious process. The challenge here

was to make the project from start to finish in an afternoon.

This project uses simple geometric shapes and

easy gingerbread and royal icing recipes to make a charming

trio of birdhouses in just a few hours. The process

consists of five simple steps: making up a batch of gingerbread

dough, and rolling it out on baking sheets, tracing

around the templates to make the shapes, baking the gingerbread

pieces, "gluing" the pieces of the birdhouses

together using royal icing, and adding decorative icing

squiggles, swirls, and dots.

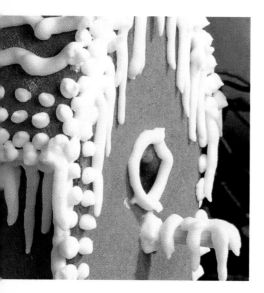

Materials

Yields three gingerbread birdhouses

- 8tbsps butter, softened
- ½ cup (125ml) dark brown sugar, lightly packed
- ¼ cup (60ml) unsulfured molasses
- ¼ cup (60ml) dark corn syrup
- 3½ cups (875ml) flour, sifted
- 1tsp baking soda
- 2tsps ground ginger
- 1tsp ground cinnamon
- ¼tsp ground nutmeg
- ¼tsp ground cloves
- ¼tsp ground cardamom
- ¼tsp salt
- ¼ cup (60ml) water

ROYAL ICING:

- 3 egg whites
- 2 cups (500ml) confectioners' sugar

YOU'LL ALSO NEED:

templates (see page 187); lightweight cardboard; pencil with new eraser; tracing paper; paper plates; ballpoint pen; ruler; scissors; two rimless baking sheets; serrated plastic knife; bath towel; two large resealable freezer bags; four or five sandwich-size freezer bags; twist ties; sifter; electric mixer; wooden rolling pin; kitchen knife; and two toothpicks.

Instructions

MAKING THE GINGERBREAD DOUGH

1. *Cream butter and sugar.* In large mixing bowl, using electric mixer on medium speed, cream together butter and brown sugar. Add molasses and corn syrup and continue mixing until well combined.

2. *Mix dry ingredients with creamed mixture.* Sift together dry ingredients. Add to sugar mixture, a little at a time, alternating with water and mixing until well combined.

3. *Shape and refrigerate dough.* Lightly flour hands and gather dough into ball. Divide ball in half and place each half into a large self-closing plastic bag. Shape dough inside bags into rough squares using palms of hands. Close bags and refrigerate at least 1 hour. While dough is chilling, prepare royal icing.

PREPARING THE ROYAL ICING

Clean beaters and bowl, then set mixer on high speed and beat egg whites until fluffy. Add confectioners' sugar, about ½ cup (125ml) at a time, until icing is stiff. Test icing by running kitchen knife blade through it. When walls of cut area hold, icing is ready. Transfer icing to four or five sandwich-size resealable freezer bags, close each bag with twist tie, and refrigerate until ready to use.

CONSTRUCTING THE BIRDHOUSES

1. *Make templates.* Using pencil, trace birdhouse templates (see page 187) onto tracing paper. Lay tracing paper upside down on cardboard or poster board. Using ruler and ballpoint pen, go over traced lines, pressing firmly to make impression on cardboard. Remove tracing paper and darken impressions with pencil. Cut along lines to make templates.

2. *Preheat oven and roll out dough.* Preheat oven to 325° F (170° C). Grease baking sheets with butter and lightly dust with flour. Take dough from refrigerator and remove from bags; place on baking sheets. Let dough warm up for about 10 minutes before rolling. Put thick bath towel on work surface, then put one baking sheet on top of towel. Lightly flour rolling pin, then roll out dough to ¼in (6mm) thick, or until it covers baking sheet. Repeat with second piece of dough.

3. *Cut out templates.* Lay templates on top of dough and cut around

Making the Birdhouses

A. Lay the templates on the dough and cut around each shape.

B. Break a toothpick in half for a perch. Make a hole above the perch with a pencil eraser.

C. Squeeze a vertical line of icing on each inside edge of each back piece, then adhere the sides.

D. Position each house on top of the base, add icing, and press to adhere.

E. To attach the roof, squeeze a line of icing on the tops of the walls, and press roof pieces to adhere.

F. Squeeze the icing onto the roof to suggest accumulated snow and icicles.

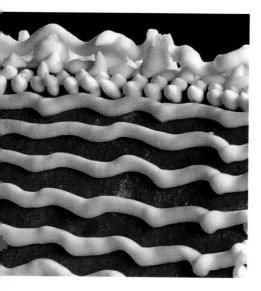

designer's tip

* * * * * * *

If you need to make repairs or
corrections on any of the icing
swirls or squiggles, carefully
remove any big globs with a
damp cotton swab. Dip a second
cotton swab in water and rub
it over the remaining icing to
partially dissolve it, then dab the
rest away with a dry cotton swab.

each using serrated plastic knife (see illustration A, facing page). For each house, cut two front/back pieces, two side pieces, and three roof/base pieces (total twenty one pieces for three houses). Repeat process with second piece of dough or re-roll scraps and repeat.

4. *Make holes for perches.* Break toothpicks in half and cut off sharp ends with scissors. Using template as reference, stick broken end into each front piece to serve as a perch. Use new pencil eraser to make hole above perch, moving in a circular pattern until desired size is reached (illustration B).

5. *Bake and cool gingerbread.* Bake gingerbread pieces for 10–15 minutes. Test for doneness by inserting kitchen knife blade into one piece; if blade comes out clean, gingerbread is done. If necessary, trim any rough edges or separate pieces that have run together. Let gingerbread cool at least 20 minutes.

6. *Test icing.* Remove one bag of icing from refrigerator. Using scissors, make ⅛in (3mm)-diagonal snip across one bottom corner of bag. Squeeze bag gently so icing flows down to cut area. Squeeze small amount of icing onto paper plate to test how quickly it flows and what shape the beaded line takes. If necessary, cut larger opening.

7. *Attach back and side pieces.* Squeeze a vertical line of icing down each edge of each back piece from roofline to floor. Stand back piece upright, and using these lines of icing as glue, attach two side pieces to back (illustration C).

8. *Attach front piece to sides and back.* Squeeze a vertical line of icing down each edge of each front piece. Stand front piece upright and attach to three-sided assembly from previous step using icing as glue, then let set about 5 minutes.

9. *Attach house to base.* Carefully lift each partially assembled house and set on base. Note position, then lift away and pipe icing onto base to correspond to house bottom. Position house on top of icing and press very gently to adhere (illustration D). Pipe icing around base of each birdhouse as desired to suggest snowbanks.

10. *Attach and decorate roof.* To attach roof, squeeze a continuous line of icing around top edges of walls and position roof pieces one at a time. Gently press into icing, then let set about 10 minutes (illustration E). (Don't worry about making perfect joints, as the royal icing will conceal any gaps.) Squeeze icing onto roof sides and peak to suggest shingles, accumulated snow, or icicles, or to hide cracks.

11. *Decorate sides, front, and back pieces.* To make dots, squeeze a tiny blob of icing into one spot, then lift the bag directly upwards. To make squiggles, squeeze a small amount of icing out of the bag's tip to start the flow, then move the bag from side to side as you squeeze a continuous flow of icing. To make icicles (which should be put on last), position tip of bag at point where you want icicle to hang, then squeeze icing until a ¼–½ in (6–12mm) line of icing hangs down (illustration F).

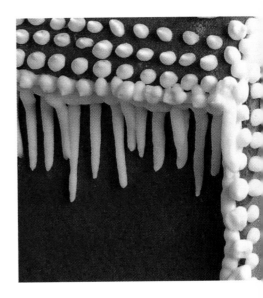

TIPS ON ROLLING AND CUTTING DOUGH

Rolling out and cutting the dough directly on the baking sheets eliminates the need to move the pieces of dough around, and helps you avoid tearing or distorting them. When cutting out the dough, choose the area that is smoothest and most free of cracks for the birdhouse roof, since these pieces are the most visible.

ASSEMBLY TIPS

Use a serrated plastic knife to cut out the pieces. The blunt, thick blade creates a separation between the cut pieces and the serrated blade prevents the dough from stretching as you cut it. The blade of a regular kitchen knife is too thin, and the pieces would run together when you bake them. (If this occurs, anyway, run a knife blade between the pieces to separate them after they've been baked, while the dough is still hot.) When assembling the house, turn each piece so the side that faced the cookie sheet during baking is on the inside of the house, as the other side will generally be smoother. (If necessary, you can conceal uneven texture or defects with the royal icing decorations.)

WORKING WITH ICING

Mix up the royal icing, then store it in four or five sandwich-size self-closing freezer bags secured with twist ties. The bags have to withstand considerable pressure when you squeeze them to pipe the icing, so be sure to use freezer-weight bags rather than ordinary plastic bags, and be sure to tie the tops with twist ties instead of relying on the self-closing, otherwise the bags may burst or split open. Chilled icing is easier to pipe and direct, so store the bags in the refrigerator until you're ready to use them. Your hands will warm up the bags a little as you pipe, so the last icing to come out will be harder to control and may appear drippy. If this begins to happen, switch to another chilled bag of icing.

Court Jester Stocking

This striking Christmas stocking

stands upright on a mantel. The stocking's bootlike

design relies on two tricks to

keep it upright. First, the walls of the stocking

use two layers of dupioni silk

with fusible knit interfacing and lightweight

batting in between, which gives

the fabric extra body. Second, the stocking features

a chipboard sole covered with silk fabric

to stabilize the bottom.

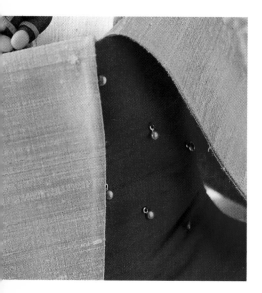

Materials

- *⅓yd (.3m) 45in (1.2m)-wide red silk dupioni (for stocking body)*
- *⅝yd (.6m) 45in (1.1m)-wide gold silk dupioni (for lining, cuff, and insole)*
- *⅔yd (.7m) 60in (1.5m)-wide fusible nylon tricot knit interfacing*
- *½yd (.5m) 36in (1m)-wide fusible woven rayon interfacing*
- *⅓yd (.3m) 45in (1.1m)-wide light-weight batting*
- *Six ½in (12mm)-diameter silver thread balls with self-loops*
- *Matching thread*
- *8 x 10in (20.5 x 25cm) piece two-ply chipboard*
- *Pearl cotton (or similar cord)*
- *White craft glue*
- *Spray adhesive*

YOU'LL ALSO NEED:

patterns (see page 185); sewing machine; iron; small dressmaker's ham (or tightly rolled hand towel); rotary cutter; acrylic grid ruler; self-healing cutting mat; sewing shears; beading needle; embroidery needle; hand-sewing needle; straight pins; point turner; waxed paper; a heavy book; tracing paper; pencil; and scissors.

OTHER ITEMS, IF NECESSARY:

approximately 110 brass charms.

Instructions

1. *Prepare patterns and fabrics.* Prepare stocking, cuff, and insole patterns (see page 185), then cut out with scissors. Using rotary cutter, grid ruler, and cutting mat, rough-cut the following items: From red silk fabric, cut two 12 x 17in (30.5 x 43cm) rectangles for stocking, with longer edge along crosswise grain. From gold silk fabric, cut two 12 x 17in (30.5 x 43cm) rectangles for lining, four 8½ x 10½in (21.5 x 26.5cm) rectangles for cuff, and two 5 x 11in (12.5 x 28cm) rectangles for insole, with longer edges along crosswise grain. From fusible knit interfacing, cut four 12 x 17in (30.5 x 43cm) rectangles. From lightweight batting, cut two 12 x 17in (30.5 x 43cm) rectangles and one 5 x 11in (12.5 x 28cm) rectangle. From fusible woven interfacing, cut four 8½ x 10½in (21.5 x 26.5cm) rectangles. Following manufacturer's directions, fuse knit interfacings to wrong side of same-size red and gold rectangles.

2. *Sew stocking.* On flat work surface, stack the following 12 x 17in (30.5 x 43cm) pieces: one batting, one red silk right side up, one red silk right side down, and one batting. Align long edges at top, and pin through all four layers to prevent shifting. Position stocking pattern on stack, aligning straight edges at top, and pin to top batting only. Using pattern as template, machine-stitch curved edges all around; leave top straight edge open. To improve accuracy at toe, change to shorter stitch length. Unpin and remove pattern. Trim batting as close to stitching as possible on both sides, then trim seam allowance ⅜in (9mm) from stitching all around (see illustration A, facing page). Clip curves, turn right side out, and press lightly.

3. *Sew lining.* Place two gold silk linings right sides together and align long top edges. Pin stocking pattern to fabric as above. Machine-stitch curved edges all around, leaving opening for turning between dots. To reinforce seam, stitch ⅛in (3mm) inside previous stitching. Trim off excess fabric (illustration B). Clip curves, turn right side out, and press lightly.

4. *Sew cuffs.* Separate fusible woven interfacing cuffs into two pairs. Place one pair interfacing cuffs on wrong side of 8½ x 10½in (21.5 x 26.5cm) gold silk cuff, align top straight edges, and fuse following manufacturer's directions. Place this cuff and a plain gold silk cuff right sides together and pin. Set machine to short stitch length (25 stitches per inch). Using interfacing as a template, pin then stitch cuff points all around edge of interfacing; leave top straight edge open. Trim seam allowance ½in (12mm) from stitching all around (illustration C). Using scissors,

Making the Court Jester Stocking

A. Stitch the stocking outline and trim off the excess fabric.

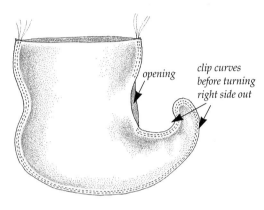

opening

clip curves before turning right side out

B. Sew the lining in the same way, but leave an opening for turning.

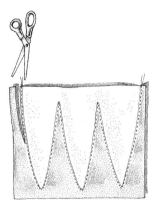

C. Use an interfacing template to sew a cuff with points.

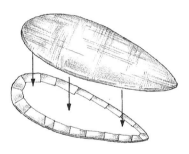

D. Layer chipboard, batting, and silk fabric to assemble the insole.

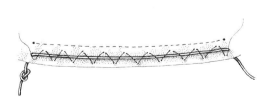

E. Enclose a cord in a zigzag casing along the stocking lower edge.

F. Draw the cord to gather the lower edge to about 5¾in (14.5cm).

designer's tip

✳ ✳ ✳ ✳ ✳ ✳ ✳

To give the stocking added
interest, tiny charms are sewn
in a random pattern over the
outside surface. If you select
fabric with a pattern, you
can skip this step.

carefully clip into allowance at inner points. Press open top seam allowance (makes turning easier), trim full seam allowance ⅛in (3mm) from stitching, and trim across lower points. Turn cuff right side out, gently push out points with point turner, and press. Repeat process for second cuff.

5. *Make insole.* On chipboard, mark one large and one small insole (see pattern); cut out both pieces with craft knife. Following manufacturer's directions and working in a well-ventilated area, apply spray adhesive to larger sole. Set sole face down on 5 x 11in (12.5 x 28cm) piece of batting, then press to adhere. Use scissors to trim excess even with sole edge. Lightly spray batting surface of sole, then press sole batting side down on wrong side of 5 x 11in (12.5 x 28cm) gold silk. Trim fabric ¾in (18mm) beyond sole edge all around; clip into allowance every ⅜in (9mm) to make tabs. Apply thin bead white craft glue to edge of sole, fold tabbed allowance onto wet glue area, and press down. Set waxed paper on top, and weight with heavy book. Repeat process to cover smaller insole with remaining gold fabric, but omit batting. Let both pieces dry thirty minutes. Glue soles back to back (illustration D), weight with book, and let dry one hour.

6. *Gather sole of stocking.* Cut 10in (25cm) length of pearl cotton cord. Turn stocking inside out, lay cord along sole seam allowance, and zigzag over cord between dots; leave ends loose (illustration E). Thread one end of cord into embroidery needle, then draw needle into seam allowance near dot, and knot end of cord. Draw up cord from other end, gathering sole to 5¾in (14.5cm), knot end, and clip off excess (illustration F). Turn stocking right side out. Insert small dressmaker's ham or tightly rolled hand towel into stocking, then press gathered sole from right side. Repeat process to gather sole of lining.

7. *Sew charms to stocking.* Thread beading needle with red thread. Beginning about 1in (2.5cm) below top edge of stocking, sew row of five charms 1¾-2in (4.5-5cm) apart; for handcrafted look, avoid precise spacing or measuring. Stitch a second row of five charms approximately 1in (2.5cm) below first row, staggering placement diagonally for subtle diamond pattern. Continue sewing charms in staggered rows, stopping approximately 2in (5cm) from bottom seam. Set insole into stocking, stand stocking upright, and check charm placement. Remove insole. Sew additional charms to toe and any bare areas (illustration G). Repeat process to sew charms to other side.

8. *Assemble stocking.* Place wrong side of one cuff against right side of stocking, top edges aligned, then raise cuff ½in (12mm) beyond stocking top edge to align cuff and stocking stitching lines (see patterns). Machine-baste 1in (2.5cm) from cuff edge along stitching line (illustration H). Repeat process to baste second cuff to opposite side. Trim excess batting close to stitching, but do not trim fabric. Turn stocking wrong side out. Set lining into stocking, right sides together and side seams matching, align top edge of lining ½in (12mm) below cuff edge, and pin. Stitch 1in (2.5cm) from upper edge of cuff, along machine basting; do not trim seam allowances (illustration I). Turn right side out through lining opening and slip-stitch opening closed (illustration J). Press upper edge of stocking, then drop lining down inside stocking. Hand-tack silver ball to each cuff point. Set insole into stocking (illustration K).

designer's tip
* * * * * * *
Use a series of coordinated stockings to decorate a sideboard or mantel, or use one stocking alone as the central focus of a decorative centerpiece.

Finishing the Court Jester Stocking

cuff is ½in above stocking

G. Sew on the charms, insert the insole, and stand the stocking upright.

H. Machine-baste each cuff to the top edge of the stocking.

I. Sew the lining to the stocking, trapping the cuff in the seam.

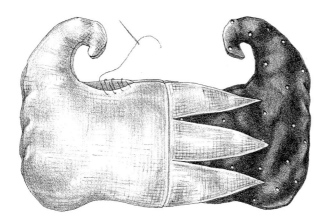

J. Turn both fabrics right side out, and slip-stitch the opening closed.

K. Tuck the lining inside the stocking. Tack silver balls to each cuff and insert the insole.

Greeting Cards and Gift Tags

 Handmade gift cards and tags are small extras with impact. In many ways they are extensions of your gifts and of the relationship between you and the person to whom you are giving. As this chapter demonstrates, making your own greeting cards and gift tags need not be time consuming or difficult. You can make your own package tags, for example, by rubber stamping images on store-bought tags. Creating a jacketed greeting card, on the other hand, is as simple as folding and cutting paper to match a special image.

Cut-Window Collage Cards

These mixed-media cards are tiny gifts

unto themselves. Assemble the cards by folding a cover

and inside pages from heavy paper, cutting

out a window in the cover, and suspending trinkets

on wire inside the window. You can hang

any number of different items in the window, from

charms, buttons, and beads to found objects

or disassembled jewelry. A colored paper background

provides a contrasting surface for

offsetting these objects within the cutout window.

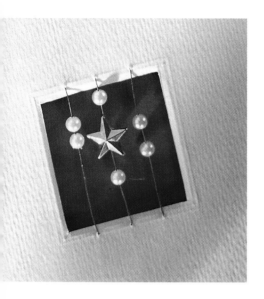

Materials

Yields three 5 x 6in (12.5 x 15cm) cards

- *Assorted trinkets: buttons, pearls, charms, beads, etc.*
- *28-gauge silver or gold spool wire*
- *1 sheet each 18 x 24in (46 x 61cm) medium- and heavy-weight water-color paper*
- *18 x 10in (46 x 25cm) sheet medium-weight colored drawing paper*
- *Thin metallic cord*
- *Double-sided tape*

YOU'LL ALSO NEED:

steel ruler; craft knife; clear acrylic grid ruler; wood stylus; pencil; self-healing cutting mat; embroidery needle; wire cutters or old scissors; and graph paper.

designer's tip
* * * * * * * *

For variation on these card designs, consider gilding the area behind the trinkets; making two embossed borders around the window; or drawing freehand stars or sunburst borders around

Instructions

1. *Cut and fold paper pieces.* Working on self-healing cutting mat and using steel ruler and craft knife, draft and cut the following pieces for each card: one 5 x 24in (12.5 x 61cm) card cover from heavier-weight watercolor paper; one 5 x 11in (12.5 x 28cm) inside page from lighter-weight watercolor paper; and one 4⅞ x 5¾ (12.3 x 14.5cm) window background from colored drawing paper. Fold cover in fourths: First, fold in half crosswise, then unfold, lay flat, and fold each end to within ¹⁄₁₆in (1.5mm) of middle fold (see illustration A, facing page). Fold inside sheet in half crosswise.

2. *Cut window.* Draft 5 x 6in (12.5 x 15cm) rectangle on graph paper to represent folded card size. Using grid as guide, arrange one or more trinkets in center of rectangle, then draft smaller rectangle (no larger than 2in [5cm] square) around them to represent window. Tape graph paper rectangle to center of panel 3 of cover (illustration B), position both pieces of paper on self-healing cutting mat, then use steel ruler and craft knife to cut out window through both layers.

3. *Emboss window, then wire trinkets to window.* Using wood stylus and grid ruler, emboss a border around window ³⁄₁₆in (5mm) beyond cut edges. For "valley" effect, emboss border on right side; emboss on wrong side for raised effect. Wrap wire securely around trinket(s) or thread through holes, then position within window so wire ends extend at least 1in (2.5cm) beyond opening. Clip off excess wire. Using embroidery needle, pierce hole on embossed border for each wire end, then thread wire through on right side. Turn cover face down and tape wire ends on wrong side using double-sided tape (illustration C).

4. *Add pages and background.* Place folded sheet inside cover so folds butt, then unfold and lay flat. Using needle and ruler, pierce two holes along fold line 1¼in (3.2cm) and 1¾in (4.5cm) from each outside edge (for a total of four holes). Thread needle with 9in (23cm) length of metallic cord. Starting at outside cover, sew cover and pages together (illustration D). Tie ends together in overhand knot and trim excess. Slip colored background between window panel and inside flap and press gently to adhere to tape (illustration E).

Making the Cut-Window Card

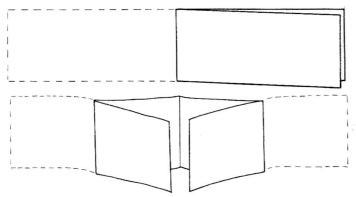

A. To make the card's cover, fold a strip of medium-weight watercolor paper in fourths.

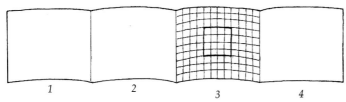

B. Use a graph paper template to cut a window opening in cover panel number 3.

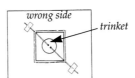

C. Tape the wire ends down on the wrong side of the window with double-sided tape.

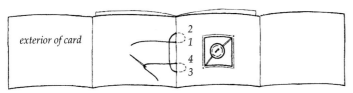

D. Make four holes along the folded spine and sew in the inside page using metallic thread.

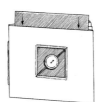

E. Slip a colored paper insert behind the cut-out window opening.

MAKING YOUR OWN ENVELOPES

It's easy to make your own envelopes. Using illustration G as a reference, sketch out a similar shape about ⅜in (9mm) larger all around than your cards (the extra space will allow for the card's thickness). Cut along the solid lines and fold along the dashed lines. To make the envelope, start by folding in the side flaps. Then put glue on the side edges of the bottom flap, fold it up, and adhere it in place. To seal the envelope, turn down the top flap and adhere it with glue or double-sided tape.

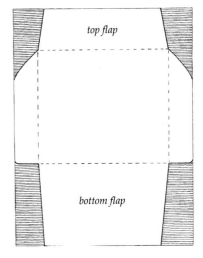

Cut along the solid lines and fold along the dashed lines.

Folded Paper Envelopes

These elegant folded paper envelopes are designed to house flat gifts

such as theater tickets, gift certificates, or photographs.

You can create them from any type of art paper, so it is simple

to customize the wrapping to suit the occasion.

The envelope comprises two parallelograms, which are stacked

perpendicular to one another like a pinwheel.

To open and close the card, the four pointed ends fold inward

and overlap, much the way a carton lid closes.

In this project, where papers are glued together, it is important

that the paper grain runs in the same direction

to prevent buckling and warping.

Materials

- *Medium- to heavyweight art papers*
- *Glue stick*

OTHER ITEMS, AS NEEDED:
- *Metallic elastic cord*
- *Buttons*
- *Tassels*
- *Sealing wax and seal*

YOU'LL ALSO NEED:
dowel; craft knife; clear acrylic grid ruler; self-healing cutting mat; scissors; and ruler.

designer's tips
✳ ✳ ✳ ✳ ✳ ✳ ✳

If you plan to mail the folded paper envelope and you've trimmed it with three-dimensional items such as buttons or wax seals, be sure to use a padded mailing envelope.

✳ ✳ ✳ ✳ ✳ ✳ ✳

Select the envelope papers to match the occasion of the enclosed gift. Gold and white papers are good for more formal invitations, such as weddings; earth-toned papers, such as taupe and ivory, for more informal gifts.

Instructions

1. *Cut rectangles.* Determine finished (folded) envelope size, e.g., 5in (12.5cm) square. Multiply one edge measurement by 3 to determine rectangle size, e.g., 5 x 15in (12.5 x 38cm). Choose two contrasting art papers for envelope exterior and a third, slightly lighter paper, for envelope liner. Using grid ruler, craft knife, and cutting mat, cut one 5 x 15in (12.5 x 38cm) rectangle from first paper, long edge parallel to paper grain. Repeat to cut second rectangle from contrasting paper, long edge perpendicular to paper grain.

2. *Cut liner rectangle.* Subtract ⅛in (3mm) all around from folded envelope size, e.g., 4¾in (12cm) square. To determine size of liner, multiply one liner edge measurement by 2½ and round up to nearest quarter inch, e.g., 4¾in x 2½ (12cm x 2½) equals 12in (30.5cm). Cut one liner rectangle measuring 4¾ x 12in (12 x 30.5cm).

3. *Cut parallelogram and fold points.* Lay one outer rectangle flat on cutting mat. Using pencil and ruler, lightly divide each long edge into thirds. To make parallelogram, align ruler diagonally from corner to nearest mark on opposite long edge, and cut with craft knife. Repeat to make parallel cut at other end of paper (see illustration A, facing page). Fold each point onto middle section, outer edges even and diagonal edges butting, to form square (illustration B), then crease with dowel. Repeat on second rectangle.

4. *Assemble envelope.* Stack two outer parallelograms, pencil marks aligned, to form pinwheel (illustration C); points should fold easily onto middle section without buckling. Join middle sections using glue stick.

5. *Fold and glue liner.* Lay liner rectangle flat. Fold one short edge toward middle and crease (illustration D). Turn over and fold other short edge under so area between folds forms a square (illustration E). Turn back over and fold down longer end to make flap (illustration F). Lay envelope flat with points opened; glue liner to center of envelope, matching paper grain.

6. *Close envelope.* Fold any point (1) onto middle section. Next, fold adjacent point (2) onto middle section (illustration G). Fold point 3 into place, then fold point 4 over 3 and insert it under 1 (illustration H).

7. *Trim envelope.* To add elastic cord, thread tassel or button onto cord, wrap cord once or twice around sleeve, and knot ends so cord fits snugly without buckling paper (illustration I).

Making the Folded Paper Envelopes

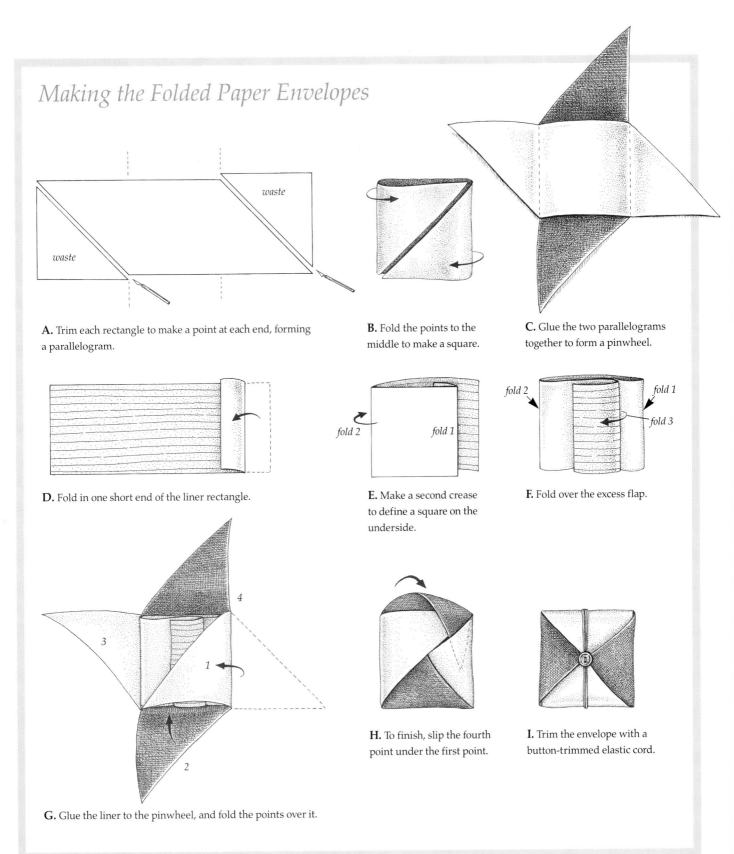

A. Trim each rectangle to make a point at each end, forming a parallelogram.

B. Fold the points to the middle to make a square.

C. Glue the two parallelograms together to form a pinwheel.

D. Fold in one short end of the liner rectangle.

E. Make a second crease to define a square on the underside.

F. Fold over the excess flap.

G. Glue the liner to the pinwheel, and fold the points over it.

H. To finish, slip the fourth point under the first point.

I. Trim the envelope with a button-trimmed elastic cord.

Scotty Dog Holiday Card

This black Scotty dog, with its red and green plaid bow

and other easy-to-apply details, is a mailable

greeting that stands on its own. With paper, ribbon, and

a few stationery supplies, you can replicate

this design or use the techniques shown here to create a diecut

card of your family pet. The success of this project,

in large part, depends on the paper you select: Choose a stiff,

heavyweight paper with a glossy black coating

on one side and a matte white surface on the other. The glossy

coating adds a slick touch to the finished card,

while the matte white backing makes a good "inside" for

writing your holiday message.

Materials

*Yields five 5¼ x 7¼in
(13.3 x 18.5cm) cards*

- *20 x 27in (51 x 68.5cm) stiff paper,
  (glossy black on one side, matte
  white on the other)*
- *8 x 10in (20.5 x 25cm) heavyweight cream-colored paper*
- *Red-and-green plaid giftwrap*
- *Five 6 x 9½in (15 x 24cm) green
  envelopes (see also "Making Your
  Own Envelopes," page 115)*
- *1⅔yds (1.5m) ¾in (1.8cm)-wide
  red plaid ribbon*
- *Five 4mm wiggle eyes*
- *Fifteen white self-adhesive dots
  or paper*
- *5¼ x 12in (13.3 x 30.5cm) green
  self-adhesive paper*

YOU'LL ALSO NEED:

*Scotty dog and miniature envelope
patterns (see page 187); craft knife;
steel ruler; self-healing cutting mat;
paper scissors; manicure scissors;
single-hole punch; bone folder or
wooden dowel; pencil; one-ply
chipboard; two or three sheets white
copier paper; newsprint; black fine-tip
permanent marker; metallic gold
felt-tip permanent marker; red felt-tip
permanent marker; glue stick; and
access to photocopier with enlarger.*

Instructions

Note: Glossy paper scratches and picks up fingerprints easily. Keep your work surface free of dust and grit and avoid touching the glossy surface unnecessarily. To handle the paper, use white paper as a buffer.

1. *Make Scotty dog and envelope templates.* Photocopy Scotty dog and miniature envelope patterns, enlarging each 200%. Rub glue stick across back of patterns, press onto chipboard, and rub gently to adhere. Lay chipboard on cutting mat. Using craft knife, cut on marked outlines; run blade against steel ruler to cut straight edges.

2. *Cut card silhouettes.* Lay black paper face down on newsprint. On white side, draft five 5⅜ x 15in (13.7 x 38cm) rectangles. Cut out rectangles using scissors. Fold each rectangle in half crosswise, white side facing in, and crease using bone folder. Place one folded rectangle on mat. Set Scotty template on top, aligning dashed line (at dog's backside) with folded edge (see illustration A, facing page). To cut out card, run craft knife blade along edge of template, pressing firmly to cut through both layers. Cut from two directions to make sharp points and notches. Smooth curled edges with bone folder, using separate sheet of white paper as buffer. Repeat process to cut five cards.

3. *Add ribbon collar.* For each card, cut one 4½in (11.5cm) and one 7in (18cm) length of ribbon. Wrap shorter ribbon around dog's neck (card front only), and glue to secure. Fold one end of 7in (18cm) ribbon into 2in (5cm) loop, glue securely, then wrap remainder around middle and glue. Glue mock bow to collar (illustration B). Repeat process for each card.

4. *Cut miniature envelope.* Lay heavyweight cream paper on cutting mat, lay miniature envelope template on paper, and trace around edges with pencil. Cut out using craft knife and steel ruler. Run gold metallic marker along steel ruler and diagonal edges to highlight envelope flap. Fold envelope on dashed lines (illustration C) so gold-edged flap falls outside. Using manicure scissors, cut jaw slit (see Scotty dog pattern, page 187) on card front. Slip envelope in behind lower jaw, then glue to jaw and foreleg. Repeat process for each card.

5. *Add wiggle eye.* Press hole punch through white self-adhesive paper to make slightly smaller dot. Remove backing and press smaller dot onto card front at eye position (see Scotty dog pattern, page 187). Glue wiggle eye to lower area of white dot. Repeat for each card.

6. *Add holly and berries.* For holly, cut two 1¼ x ¾in (3.2 x 1.8cm) ovals from green self-adhesive paper. To make prickly holly leaves, cut edge of oval all around with hole punch. For berries, use red marker to color two white self-adhesive dots. Press hole punch through one red dot to cut slightly smaller dot. Peel backing from holly leaves and berries and press onto card below bow (illustration D). Touch black marker to each berry near edge to mark stem depression. Repeat for each card.

7. Line mailing envelope. Open one green mailing envelope, lay it flat on plaid giftwrap, and trace around edge with pencil. Cut out liner with scissors, trim side edges slightly, and slip into mailing envelope. Fold down envelope flap, creasing liner as you go. Trim flap edges of liner to fall about ½in (12mm) inside envelope flap, clearing gummed section. Secure liner to envelope flap and interior using glue stick. Make one lined envelope per card.

designer's tip
✶ ✶ ✶ ✶ ✶ ✶ ✶
MAKING YOUR PET GREETING CARD
This card design can be for other dog breeds. Start by locating a silhouette of your dog's breed to make a pattern. Consider tracing stencils, images in dog magazines, appliqué patterns, photographs, or the like. For this card design to work, the card's fold should appear at the dog's backside. This may require some modification to the pattern. Once you've created your pattern, select paper that matches your dog's coat color, or layer paper to create multicolor designs.

Making the Scotty Dog Card

A. Lay a cardboard template on folded paper to cut each Scotty card.

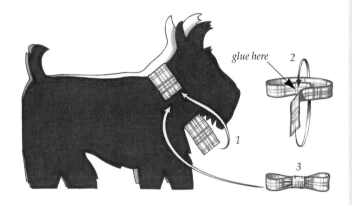

B. Glue a plaid ribbon with a mock bow around the Scotty's neck.

C. Glue a miniature envelope to the Scotty's jaw and foreleg.

D. Finish with a wiggle eye and self-adhesive holly leaves and berries.

Laminated Greeting Cards

These layered greeting cards require

only four basic materials—paper, envelopes, a piece

of textured stock, and a decorative image—

yet the resulting designs are elegant and distinctive.

To get started, choose the card paper.

Then experiment with images and overlay papers

until you find a combination that

you like. Finally, select the text for your greeting.

Materials

Makes twenty 5 x 7in (12.5 x 18cm) cards with envelopes

SEASON'S GREETINGS CARD

■ *1 sheet 24 x 36in (61 x 91cm) textured white lace paper*

■ *Season's Greetings type (see page 127)*

HAPPY NEW YEAR CARD

■ *1 sheet 24 x 36in (61 x 91cm) gold-flecked mulberry lace paper*

■ *20 skeleton leaves, approximately 3½ x 5in (9 x 12.5cm)*

■ *Happy New Year type (see page 127)*

YOU'LL ALSO NEED:

twenty sheets laser paper, plus extra sheets for testing; twenty 5¼ x 7¼in (13.3 x 18.5cm) taupe envelopes; access to photocopier; spray adhesive; deckle-edging scissors; rubber stamp with 2½in (6.5cm) star motif; pigment stamp pad with gold ink; gold embossing powder; toaster or toaster oven; self-healing gridded cutting mat; clear acrylic grid ruler; steel ruler; craft knife; glue stick; pencil; scissors; and newsprint.

Instructions

1. *Create card template.* To make 5 x 7in (12.5 x 18cm) card template to fit 5¼ x 7¼in (13.3 x 18.5cm) envelope, fold sheet of laser paper in half crosswise, lay it flat with fold at left, and lightly draft perpendicular lines 5in (12.5cm) from folded edge and 7in (18cm) from top edge, or ¼in (6mm) smaller than envelope dimensions. Photocopy type. If using "Season's Greetings" type, cut type in two pieces with craft knife. Using glue stick and clear grid ruler, center and affix "Season's" 1¼in (3.2cm) below top edge and "Greetings" 1¼in (3.2cm) above bottom penciled edge (see illustration A, facing page). If using "Happy New Year" type, cut out type using craft knife. Using glue stick and clear grid ruler, center and affix type to card template 1¼in (3.2cm) from top edge.

2. *Print cards.* Unfold template, lay face down on photocopier, and load laser paper, including extras, into paper tray. Print one copy on standard setting. If edge of message shows up as shadow, change to lighter setting and reprint until clear. When setting is correct, print twenty copies.

3. *Fold and cut cards.* Fold each printed sheet in half, type facing out, as for template. With gridded mat underneath as guide, use steel ruler and craft knife to trim off side and bottom edges of each card through both layers as marked (illustration B). Use deckle-edging scissors to trim right edge of each card front.

FINISH SEASON'S GREETINGS CARD

1. *Stamp and emboss star.* Emboss cards in assembly-line style, first stamping star design on center of each card, then sprinkling embossing powder on top while ink is still wet (illustration C). Hold each card over heated toaster or open toaster oven set to 350° F (180° C) for 20–30 seconds to activate embossing powder. (Also see illustrations F and G in "Rubber Stamp Gift Tags," page 135).

2. *Affix lace paper overlay.* Using steel ruler and craft knife, cut twenty 4 x 6in (10 x 15cm) overlays from lace paper. Working in well-ventilated work area, lay overlays flat on newsprint so edges do not touch, then position additional newsprint around to catch overspray. Spray overlays lightly with adhesive. Affix overlays to cards by touching down one short edge so corners are square, then lower remainder of overlay onto face of card and press gently (do not rub) with palm (illustration D).

FINISH HAPPY NEW YEAR CARD

1. *Affix skeleton leaves to cards.* Lay skeleton leaves face down on newsprint and spray lightly with adhesive, as in step 2 of Season's Greetings card. To affix each leaf to card front, hold it in position ½in (12mm) above card and touch down on surface.

2. *Affix lace paper overlay.* Using steel ruler and craft knife, cut twenty 4 x 6in (10 x 15cm) overlays from mulberry lace paper. Lay overlays flat on fresh newsprint and spray lightly with adhesive; in order to affix overlays to cards, touch down one short edge so corners are square, then lower remainder of overlay onto face of card and press gently (do not rub) with palm (illustration E).

designer's tip
✳ ✳ ✳ ✳ ✳ ✳ ✳
If you have a computer, you can "typeset" your own greeting card messages. The text should be in horizontal rather than upright format.

Making the Cards

A. Affix the greeting type within the card area using a glue stick.

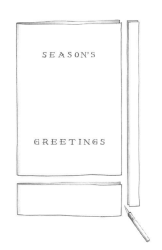

B. Photocopy twenty cards onto blank laser paper, then fold each card in half and trim the edges.

C. Use a rubber stamp and embossing powder to create a raised star on the card's front.

D. Use a light coat of spray adhesive to affix the lace paper over the star.

E. Use spray adhesive to affix a skeletonized leaf and a lace paper overlay to the card's front.

H A P P Y   N E W   Y E A R !
S E A S O N ' S
G R E E T I N G S

Stationery
Greeting Cards

You can make this greeting card in a jiffy

using two store-bought materials—a sheet of stationery

and a piece of decorative card stock—plus your

own special image. Start by cutting a jacket and an inside page

for your card, then cut a window out of the jacket

to highlight your chosen image. Tie a ribbon around both folded

sheets to bind the jacket and the pages together.

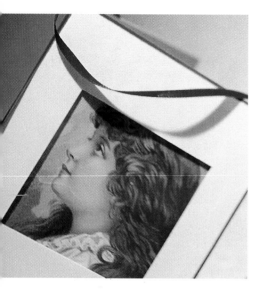

Materials

- *Small printed images or photographs*
- *Single-fold sheets of stationery with matching envelopes*
- *Card stock or stiff decorative or textured paper*
- *Double-faced satin ribbon or ¹⁄₁₆in (1.5mm)-diameter decorative cord*
- *Clear-drying glue*

YOU'LL ALSO NEED:
self-healing cutting mat; metal-edged ruler; scissors; craft knife; tracing paper; pencil; artist's removable tape; and ¹⁄₂in (12mm)-wide stiff paintbrush.

designer's tip
✳ ✳ ✳ ✳ ✳ ✳ ✳ ✳
Try cutting windows in different shapes or using more than one window on a single card. Ready-made templates of all shapes, available at most craft stores, make this easy.

Instructions

1. *Isolate area to appear on card.* Cover image with tracing paper. Trace around image at least ¼in (6mm) in from edges (see illustration A, facing page) using ruler for straight edges or drawing freehand for irregular shapes.

2. *Cut stock to match stationery.* Using ruler and craft knife, cut card stock to equal measurement of stationery. Then slice ¼in (6mm) off two adjacent edges of stationery.

3. *Test-fit card and envelope.* Fold both stationery and card stock in half, slip stationery inside card stock, and slip both into envelope (illustration B). If necessary, trim edge of card jacket to fit.

4. *Cut out window for image.* To mark position where image will show through jacket, remove stationery from inside jacket; open jacket flat on cutting mat with front facing up. Tape tracing from step 1 to front. Using craft knife and ruler for straight edges or cutting freehand for irregular shapes, cut through tracing paper and jacket along traced lines. Remove tracing paper, tape, and cut-out section.

5. *Position image in window.* As preparation for attaching image, reinsert stationery inside jacket (illustration C). Position image so it shows through window. Hold image down to prevent it from shifting, then carefully open jacket.

6. *Glue image to stationery.* Bend back top edge of image and apply thin bead of glue to underside (illustration D). Smooth with brush, then roll edge back into position and rub gently with clean fingertip. Repeat on bottom edge. Let dry 5-10 minutes. Clean brush with water.

7. *Attach ribbon.* Open jacket flat. Using scissors, cut ribbon or cord two times length of fold plus 5–10in (12.5–25cm). Tie around jacket and stationery at fold.

CREATE YOUR OWN IMAGE BANK

If you plan to make a large number of these greeting cards, you may want to start your own image bank so that you'll have a personal selection of art on file at all times. Keep your photographs, magazine clippings, postcards, and the like organized by subject in labeled files or folders.

Making a Display Window

designer's tip

✳ ✳ ✳ ✳ ✳ ✳ ✳

The thin decorative cord used to bind the card is more than a closure—it's also a design element. It can be used to bring out or contrast a color in the highlighted image or, if patterned or textured, take on emphasis of its own.

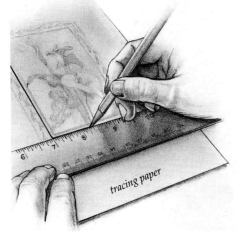

A. Trace around the image at least ¼in (6mm) in from its edges. Use a ruler for straight edges or draw freehand around irregular shapes.

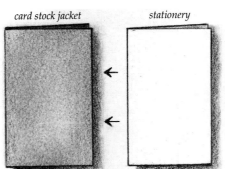
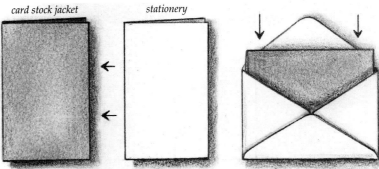

card stock jacket   stationery

B. Test-fit the card by slipping it into the envelope. Trim the edge of the card jacket to fit as necessary.

C. After cutting the window, reinsert the stationery inside the jacket and position the image so it shows through the window.

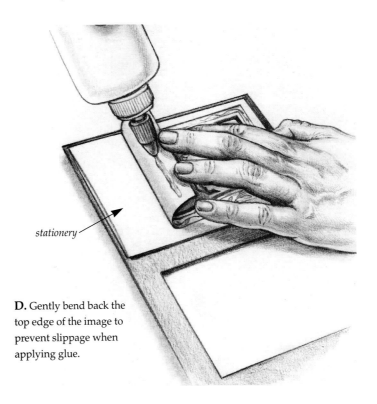

stationery

D. Gently bend back the top edge of the image to prevent slippage when applying glue.

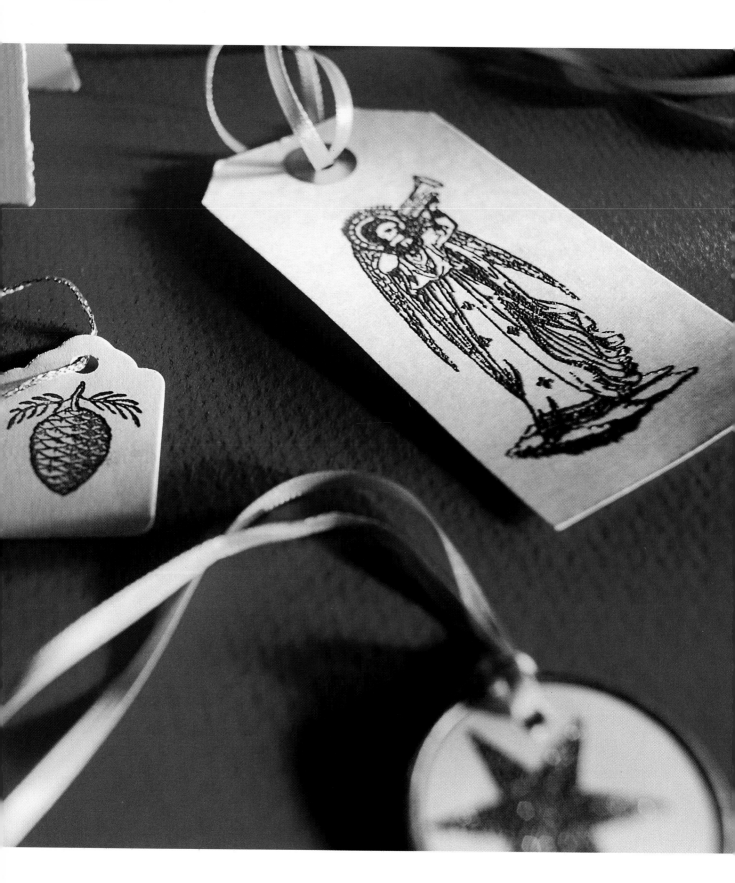

Rubber Stamp
Gift Tags

Rubber stamp gift tags and cards are a fast,

easy way to add unique finishing touches to Christmas

packages. Use a stamp that hints of the gift

under the wrapping: a strawberry stamp for your homemade

jam, for example, or a flower or garden tool stamp

if you're giving a gardening gift. You can color in your stamped

image with a complimentary marker or add sparkle

by embossing. Colorful ribbon and other stationery-store

items can lend special details to your gift tags.

Materials
- Pigment- or dye-based ink pad
- Gift tags with smooth surface
- Silk cord or other decorative ribbon

PINECONE TAG
- Rubber stamp of pinecone
- Green felt-tip permanent marker

EMBOSSED STAR AND
ANGEL TAGS
- Rubber stamp of angel or star
- Embossing powder in gold or other
  metallic color
- Hole reinforcements in gold or other
  metallic color

YOU'LL ALSO NEED:
ruler; craft knife; scissors; cotton swabs; single-hole punch; scrap paper; toaster, toaster oven, or heat gun; flat wooden tongs; and narrow brush.

Instructions
TWO-COLOR PINECONE TAG
1. Stamp pinecone. Tap stamp on brown ink pad (see illustration A, facing page). Turn stamp over and wipe brown ink off leaves with cotton swab dampened slightly with water (illustration B).

2. Color leaves. Immediately color leaves on rubber stamp green with felt-tip permanent marker (illustration C). Stamp image on center of tag (illustration D). Let dry.

3. Attach gift cord. Run gold gift cord through hole in tag and knot about 3in (7.5cm), or desired length, above ends. Trim to finish.

EMBOSSED STAR AND ANGEL TAG
1. Punch hole and stamp image. If gift tag does not have hole, use single-hole punch to make one about ⅛in (3mm) below top center of tag. Using pigment-based ink, stamp image at center of tag (illustration E).

2. Coat image with embossing powder. Place tag face up on scrap paper. While image is still wet, sprinkle with generous coating of embossing powder (illustration F). Tap off excess powder onto scrap paper and funnel back into original container. Dab off any stray particles with brush.

3. Heat powdered image. Hold tag face up over hot toaster with tongs, or set tag face up in open 350° F (180° C) toaster oven, or use heat gun (illustration G). Melt powder 20–30 seconds, then remove tag and allow to cool (illustration G). Don't overheat image, as this can cause powder to soak into paper, making image appear flat and dull.

4. Attach ribbon. Fold cord in half lengthwise and pass about 2in (5cm) through hole from front of tag to its underside. Open folded end of cord slightly to form loop, then pass remaining cord through loop. Pull to secure. For Angel tag, center opening of hole reinforcement over opening on gift tag, then affix.

EMBOSSING STAMPED IMAGES
Embossing gives the stamped image a raised, finished look. Embossing powder comes in a range of finishes, from clear and opalescent to metallic, tinsel, and enamelware. Clear and opalescent powders take on the original color of ink whereas colored opaque powders will hide the underlying color of ink. Use only pigment-based ink when embossing, as dye-based ink will not "grab" the embossing powder.

Making the Pinecone Tag

A. Ink the pinecone image on a brown ink pad.

B. Remove any brown ink from the leaves with a slightly damp cotton swab.

C. Color the leaves green with a felt-tip marker.

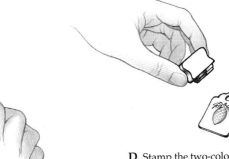

D. Stamp the two-color image.

Making the Star Tag

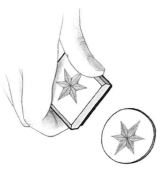

E. Stamp the image on the gift tag.

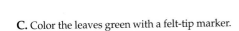

F. While the ink is still wet, sprinkle powder over the image.

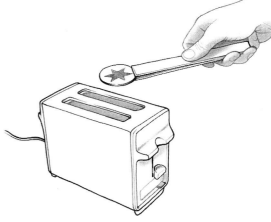

G. With wooden tongs, hold the tag face up over hot toaster.

designer's tips

✳ ✳ ✳ ✳ ✳ ✳ ✳ ✳

If you find an intricate design that would make a good rubber stamp or want to draw your own, it's possible to have a stamp commercially made. Check your local yellow pages under "Rubber Stamps" or ask a local stationery store or printer.

✳ ✳ ✳ ✳ ✳ ✳ ✳

For added interest, make a deckle edge for each tag with pinking shears.

Handmade Gifts

There is no substitute for a handmade gift, no matter how simple or small, as every stitch or drop of glue is applied with care. This chapter offers techniques for creating a wide variety of gifts for recipients of all ages. These include aromatherapeutic bath oil you can make and bottle yourself, miniature notepad books covered with suede, realistic-looking meringue mushrooms, and a pair of huggable terry cloth animals for the children on your list.

Bath Oil

Bath Oil

16 fl. oz. (300ml)

Bath Oil

Fine bath products are a much-appreciated

luxury. They make welcome Christmas gifts, because

they pamper loved ones and are reminders

of your affection long after the last tree ornament has

been put away. You can use this recipe to

make your own bath oil, then add fragrance of your

choosing with essential oils. The process is

straightforward, the tools can be found in your kitchen,

and you can buy your materials at your

local health food store.

Bath Oil

Materials

Yields 1 cup (250ml) bath oil

- *1 cup (250ml) almond or pecan oil*
- *⅛–¼tsp (0.63–1.25ml) pure vitamin E oil*
- *¼–½tsp (1.25–2.5ml) essential oil(s), plus more as desired to prolong scent*
- *Dried herbs or flowers (such as lavender sprigs or rose petals)*
- *8oz (250ml) bottle with cork stopper*
- *Concentrated candle dye (optional)*
- *Paper for labels*
- *Waxed beige cord*
- *½in (12.7mm)-wide seam binding*
- *Red sealing wax*
- *Rubber cement*

YOU'LL ALSO NEED:

measuring cup with spout; measuring spoons; microwave oven; sharp knife; chopstick; ovenproof custard cup; computer with word processing software and high-quality printer; scissors; deckle-edge scissors; ruler; newsprint; seal stamp; candle; matches; sharp knife; tweezers; scrap paper; and vegetable oil.

Instructions

1. *Mix ingredients.* Measure 1 cup (250ml) almond or pecan oil. If coloring oil, pour off about ⅛c (30ml) into custard cup. Shave three to four slivers candle dye into custard cup oil, microwave on high 10 seconds, and stir with chopstick. Repeat until dye is melted and color is evenly distributed, then return mixture to oil in measuring cup. Add vitamin E oil and essential oil(s), pour entire contents into bottle, and insert cork stopper.

2. *Mix and bottle oil.* Mix oils by gently turning bottle over and back a few times (see illustration A, facing page). Test scent by rubbing oil into skin. Add more essential oil(s) as desired to prolong scent. For visual interest, drop in dried herbs or flowers.

3. *Create label outline.* To gauge label size, cut rectangle from scrap paper, hold it against bottle, and trim to size. Using computer's word processing software, create double-bordered box about ¼in (6.4mm) smaller than sample label.

4. *Type and print label.* Type name of item and other information (ie., scent and volume) on three separate lines inside box. Center all lines, then select font and point size for each line of type. Test print on scrap paper, then print on actual paper. Cut out ¼in (6.4mm) beyond box using deckle-edge scissors.

5. *Attach label to bottle.* Lay label face down on newsprint and brush rubber cement across back. Wait one minute, or until cement is tacky, then press into position on bottle. Loop waxed cord around neck, catching ribbon at back (illustration B). Then draw both ribbon ends over top of bottle and down front. Wind cord around neck, tie off (illustration C), and cut excess. Trim ribbon ends. Apply thin coat vegetable oil to seal stamp. Light candle. Hold sealing wax over candle flame for 10 seconds, then cut ⅛in (3.2mm) coin-shaped circle from softened wax using sharp knife. Using tweezers, position wax on ribbons above label, then impress with seal stamp (illustration D).

Bottling the Bath Oil

A. Turn the bottle over and back a few times to combine the bath oil ingredients.

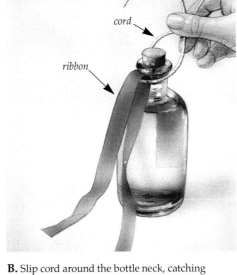

cord

ribbon

B. Slip cord around the bottle neck, catching a ribbon at the back.

C. Wrap and tie the cord to secure the ribbon.

D. Trim the ribbon ends, then top with a wax seal.

Miniature
Notepad Books

This unique stocking stuffer project

turns a mundane item, the adhesive notepad,

into an attractive and witty miniature

book. You'll need a scrap of suede for the cover,

colored paper to line the inside

jacket, an adhesive notepad for the pages,

and a leather closure.

Materials

- *Adhesive notepads in one or more following sizes: 3 x 5in (7.6 x 12.7cm), 3 x 2in (7.6 x 5.1cm), or 1½ x 2in (3.8 x 5.1cm)*
- *Scraps of suede to fit notepad(s)*
- *Medium-weight colored paper*
- *Contact cement*

YOU'LL ALSO NEED:

liner patterns (see page 186); craft knife; steel ruler; rotary cutter; self-healing cutting mat; clear acrylic grid ruler; disposable bristle brush; pencil; and newsprint.

designer's tip
✳ ✳ ✳ ✳ ✳ ✳ ✳

If you can't find suede or leather scraps for this project, you can substitute Ultrasuede. It glues well and without show-through, but because it is thinner than real suede, you will need to use thicker, stiffer liner paper to make the book sturdier.

Instructions

1. *Organize materials.* For each book, select suede scrap for cover, colored paper for liner, and adhesive notepad for pages. Suede scraps should be large enough to wrap once around pad.

2. *Cut liner.* Referring to patterns on page 186 for dimensions, lightly draft liner on colored paper. Lay colored paper on cutting mat. Using steel ruler and craft knife, cut out along solid lines and score lightly on dashed lines. Crease scorelines. Repeat process to cut one liner per pad.

3. *Glue liner to suede.* Lay suede right side down on newsprint. Lay corresponding liner on newsprint with scored side facing up. Brush contact cement onto both pieces; brush cement beyond liner edges. Let cement dry 3–5 minutes, or until surface is tacky, but not wet. Set liner on suede and press gently to adhere. Wrap glued pieces around pad, liner on inside, and crease scorelines to hug spine. Remove notepad, lay cover on mat with liner facing up, and rub to create firm bond. Use grid ruler and rotary cutter to trim suede even with liner edge all around (see illustration A, facing page). Repeat process for each pad.

4. *Attach suede thong.* Mark two short lines on front cover (see liner patterns, page 186). Slit lines by drawing craft knife against steel ruler. Using rotary cutter and grid ruler, cut ³⁄₁₆in (5mm)-wide thong from suede for each book; cut 12in (30.5cm) thongs for small books and 14in (35cm) thongs for medium and large books. Draw thong through slit and knot end (illustration B).

5. *Glue pad to cover.* Brush contact cement on inside spine of cover and spine of pad. Let dry until tacky, then press together (illustration C). Wind thong around book, and tuck in end. Repeat process for each pad.

Making the Miniature Books

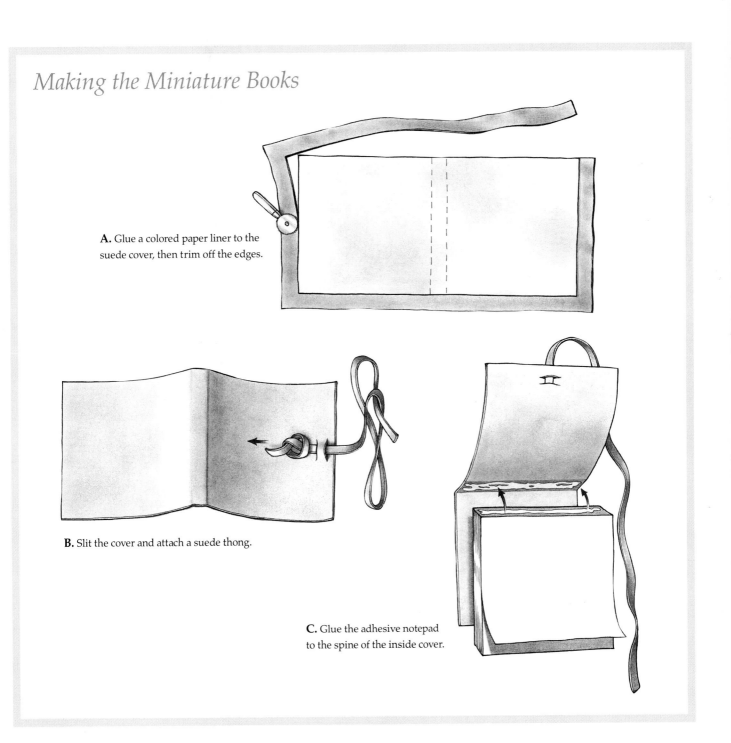

A. Glue a colored paper liner to the suede cover, then trim off the edges.

B. Slit the cover and attach a suede thong.

C. Glue the adhesive notepad to the spine of the inside cover.

Meringue Mushrooms

Though these edible meringue mushrooms

may look complicated, the hardest part about making them

is getting the correct grip on a pastry bag.

To get started, mix up a batch of meringue, which is made

from egg whites, cream of tartar, and sugar.

Pipe the mushrooms out of a large pastry bag in two pieces:

stems and caps. Next, bake these pieces

in a 200°F (100C) oven for 30 to 40 minutes, then leave

them to dry. Once dry, they are assembled

by carving a small hole on each cap underside, coating

the cap underside with melted chocolate,

and inserting a stem into the hole. As the chocolate

hardens it will hold the stem in place.

These unique edible decorations make a wonderful gift,

or a simple dessert on their own.

Materials

Yields 20–24 mushrooms

- *4 large egg whites (½ cup or 125ml)*
- *½tsp (2.5ml) cream of tartar*
- *1 cup (250ml) sugar*
- *Cocoa powder*
- *4oz (125g) semisweet chocolate chips*

YOU'LL ALSO NEED:

two large pastry bags or one large bag with coupler; ¼in (6mm)- and ½in (12mm)-diameter round pastry tips; two large baking sheets; electric mixer; glass or stainless steel mixing bowl; measuring cup; measuring spoons; fine-mesh strainer; double boiler; spatula; butter knife; paring knife; plastic or tin container with cover; waxed paper; flour; and shortening.

Note: If you're folding your own large-size pastry bags, buy the 18in (46cm) paper triangles. You can use two bags or one bag with a coupler.

designer's tip
✳ ✳ ✳ ✳ ✳ ✳ ✳

For best results, bake meringue on clear, dry day.

Instructions

1. *Mix meringue.* Lightly grease and flour baking sheets; set aside. Place egg whites in clean mixing bowl. Using electric mixer, beat at low speed; as whites begin to foam (2–3 minutes), gradually increase speed and add cream of tartar. Continue beating until whites turn opaque and form soft peaks when beaters are lifted. Beat in sugar 1tbsp (15ml) at a time, increase speed to high, and beat an additional 5–8 minutes, or until mixture is thick and firm. You should not detect any sugar granules when small amount of meringue is rubbed between your fingers.

2. *Pipe mushroom stems.* Preheat oven to 200° F (100° C). Fit pastry bag with ¼in (6mm) round tip. Transfer up to one-third of meringue to bag, and twist open end. To pipe stems, hold bag so tip is about ¾in (18mm) above baking sheet, perpendicular to surface, and squeeze gently (see illustration A, facing page). As soon as blob of meringue is about ¾in (18mm) across, lift bag straight up to form cone shape 1¼–1½in (3.2–3.8cm) high. Repeat process to pipe 20–24 cone-shaped stems; allow ½in (12mm) space between stems. Place baking sheet in oven to set shape of stems, then proceed immediately to piping mushroom caps.

3. *Pipe mushroom caps.* Fit same or new pastry bag with ½in (12mm) round tip; transfer remaining meringue to bag. To pipe caps, hold bag so tip is ¼–½in (6–12mm) above second baking sheet, perpendicular to surface. Squeeze gently and raise bag slightly to form round, puffy "pillow" about ⅝in (16mm) high and 1–1½in (2.5–3.8cm) in diameter (illustration B). Repeat process to pipe 20–24 caps; allow ½in (12mm) space between caps. Smooth peaks with a butter knife in circular motion, as if icing a cake. Place cocoa powder in strainer and sprinkle over surface of caps to suggest dirt. Place baking sheet in oven with stems. Bake 30–40 minutes, or until firm. Turn oven off, leave both trays in oven with door closed, and let dry at least 2 hours but preferably overnight.

4. *Assemble caps and stems.* Melt chocolate chips in double boiler, stirring with spatula until smooth; remove from heat. Using tip of paring knife, sculpt ¼in (6mm)-deep hole in flat side of each cap. Using butter knife, spread thin layer of melted chocolate across flat side of cap and fill hole with chocolate. Gently press pointed end of one stem into hole, and stand mushroom upright on waxed paper (illustration C). Repeat process to assemble remaining stems and caps. Let chocolate harden 1 hour.

5. *Store mushrooms.* To keep mushrooms fresh for several days, layer them between sheets of waxed paper in container; cover tightly. For longer periods, store in tightly covered plastic container in freezer.

Making the Mushrooms

A. Pipe the meringue into stem shapes. Place the baking sheet in the oven to set the shape while you pipe the caps.

B. Pipe the mushroom caps, then bake with the stems for 30 to 40 minutes, or until firm.

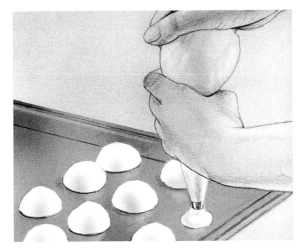

C. After baking, "glue" the cap and stem together using melted chocolate.

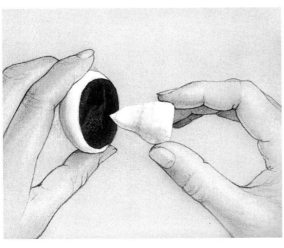

designer's tips
✳ ✳ ✳ ✳ ✳ ✳ ✳

There are a few tricks to making perfect meringues. Use fresh and cold (or defrosted) egg whites. Make the stems before the caps; the meringue is firmer when just made, helping the stems to stand straight and form a stable base for the caps.

✳ ✳ ✳ ✳ ✳ ✳ ✳

Don't make the stems too high—they will tip over. Make your first stem and measure it to make sure the height is right—1¼–1½in (3.2–3.8cm) high.

✳ ✳ ✳ ✳ ✳ ✳ ✳

Don't worry if mushrooms don't turn out alike. If they vary slightly in size and shape, they will look more realistic.

✳ ✳ ✳ ✳ ✳ ✳ ✳

If you prefer tan mushrooms to white, set your oven to 250° F (130° C). Bake the stems and caps for 45–50 minutes, then leave them in a turned-off oven to dry overnight.

✳ ✳ ✳ ✳ ✳ ✳ ✳

These mushrooms can be made in any size, and the recipe may be decreased by half or increased to any amount. Keep in mind that the cream of tartar stabilizes the egg foam, so don't use more than ⅛ teaspoon (.6ml) per egg white.

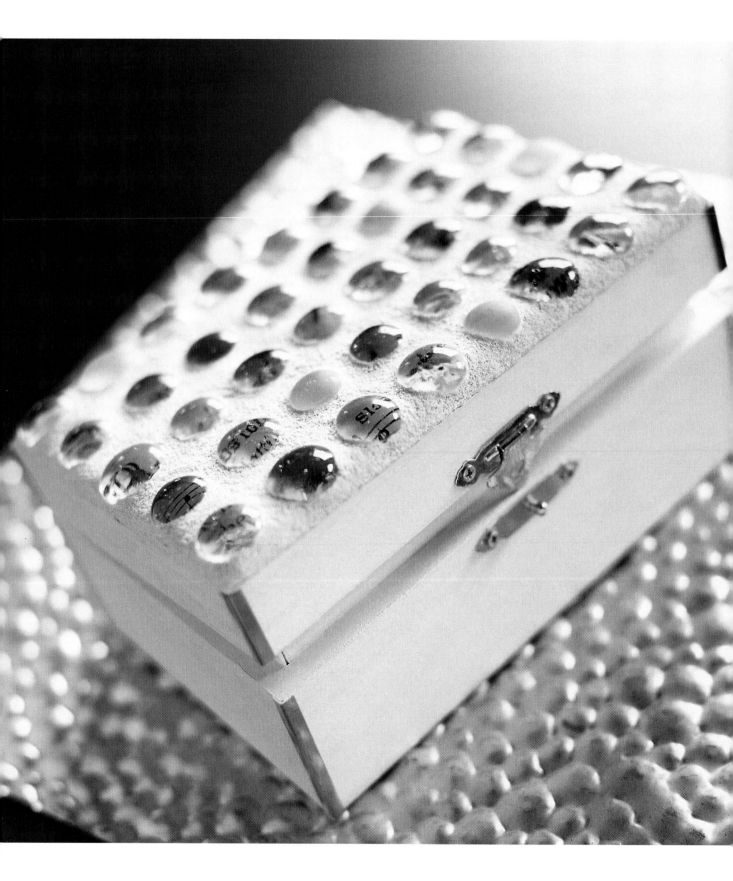

Pavé Box

This pavé box brings together several
media—a plain wooden box, paper cutouts, glass gems,
brass trim, paint, and tile grout—for a strikingly
beautiful yet subtle effect. The construction technique
is straightforward: Glue cut-out paper
squares onto the bottom of transparent glass gems.
Then glue the gems to a wooden box top,
and fill in the gaps between the gems with tile grout.
To finish the box, whitewash the outside
and add a brass catch and trim at the corners.

Materials

- Wooden box with hinged lid
- About 50 clear, flat glass "gems"
- Printed matter (books, sheet music, etc.)
- Two 10 x ⅛in (25cm x 3mm) right-angle brass strips
- Miniature brass catch
- White powdered grout (at least 1 cup [250ml])
- 2oz (60ml) white acrylic craft paint
- 2oz (60ml) metallic gold acrylic craft paint
- Glass etching cream
- Decoupage medium
- Matte acrylic sealer
- High-tack white craft glue

YOU'LL ALSO NEED:

¼in (6mm) disposable brush; ½in (12mm) soft, flat brush; 1in (2.5cm) foam brush; latex gloves; watercolor palette; disposable pint container; small paint stick; measuring cup; mug; teaspoon; 150-grit sandpaper; hacksaw; metal file; manicure scissors; fine-tip permanent marker; pencil; newspaper; newsprint; scrap cardboard; paper towels; and soft cloth.

Instructions

1. *Count and sort gems.* Arrange glass gems on box lid in grid formation, ⅛–¼in (3–6mm) apart, to determine count needed to fill surface (see illustration A, facing page). Remove gems from lid and set aside; add two or three additional gems for design flexibility.

2. *Frost and paint gems.* Set five or six gems from step 1 on scrap cardboard. Following manufacturer's instructions and wearing gloves, use ¼in (6mm) brush to spread glass etching cream across top surface of gems. Let set 10 minutes, then rinse gems under running water to reveal frosted surface. Repeat process to frost reverse side. Discard cardboard and brush; remove gloves. Select three or four gems from step 1. Using ½in (12mm) brush, paint flat underside using gold paint; color will be visible when gem is viewed from above.

3. *Select images.* Place clear gem from step 1 on printed page. Slowly move gem over surface to magnify different images, select certain words, etc. Pencil squares around interesting images, then cut out with manicure scissors (illustration B). Prepare one image per clear gem.

4. *Glue images to gems.* Lay images face up on newsprint. Using foam brush, apply thin coat decoupage medium across face of one image. Press one clear gem flat side down on image (illustration C), turn gem over, and press paper from flat side until well adhered. Examine from right side through glass to make sure all air bubbles are removed. Let dry at least 1 hour. Using manicure scissors, trim excess paper so it is even with gem edge (illustration D).

5. *Glue gems to box.* Set box on work surface with hinges at back. Arrange frosted, gold, and clear gems on box lid in grid formation, as in Step 1. Rearrange stones as needed so all words and letters face you and similar stones are not adjacent to one another. (You will have a few stones left over). Once design is set, lift one gem, apply decoupage medium to underside, and press gem back into position until adhered. Repeat process to glue down all gems (illustration E). Let dry overnight.

6. *Apply grout between gems.* Put on latex gloves and set box on several layers of newspaper. In disposable container, use paint stick to stir 1 cup (250ml) dry grout into ⅛ cup (30ml) water, or follow manufacturer's proportions and instructions. Let grout set 5 minutes, or until stiff, firm, and gritty. Spread grout over gem-covered lid using gloved finger. Poke grout down between gems, first tracing all long rows, then all short rows. Remove excess grout; keep working paths until grout surface is smooth and round gem tops are visible. At edges of lid top, mold grout flush to surface. Let dry 30 minutes. To remove grout film, polish tops of gems with soft, dry cloth. Let dry overnight, then polish gem tops again.

7. *Whitewash box.* Sand box lightly with grain to remove stray grout, then remove dust with damp paper towel. To make whitewash, squeeze 1tsp (5ml) white paint onto watercolor palette, and dilute with water until milky. Using foam brush, apply wash to outside of box, let dry 20 minutes, then open box and apply wash to inside. Prop box open and let dry 1 hour. Using foam brush, apply matte sealer to painted surfaces.

8. *Attach brass trims.* Fit brass right-angle strip onto one box corner, lower edges even. Using permanent pen, make mark on trim where lid and box meet. Saw at marks. Repeat process to mark and cut eight fittings. File sawed ends to remove burrs and to fit any gap. Using high-tack glue, affix each angle to appropriate box corner; remove oozing glue with damp paper towel. Attach catch at front using hardware provided by manufacturer (illustration F).

---

designer's tips

If you have a computer, you can generate your own type, making it easy to find exact letters or words that not only will be legible but fit under the gems perfectly.

✳ ✳ ✳ ✳ ✳ ✳

For variation, use a photocopier to enlarge or reduce found images and type, print images on different-colored papers, or create multiple images.

Making the Pavé Box

A. Select clear glass gems to form a grid on the box lid.

B. Cut out interesting bits of type or music.

C. Glue each cutout to a gem underside to magnify the image.

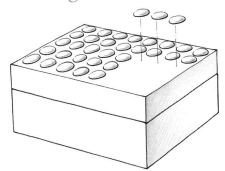

D. When the glue is dry, trim off the excess paper.

E. Glue the gems to the lid, then grout the spaces in between.

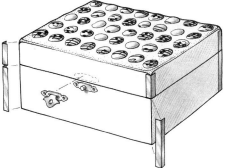

F. Whitewash the box, then attach a brass catch and trims.

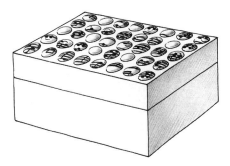

Zippered Suede Purses

These zippered purses may look complicated, but

they are actually very simple to make.

You won't need a pattern for them either: The rectangular

pieces can be measured and cut to size

using a gridded cutting mat and a rotary cutter. For

a playful design you can make the purses

using contrasting, brightly colored suede (shown here),

sateen coat lining, and a plastic zipper.

You can change the materials or colors, however,

to match an existing purse, to suit

the time of year, or with a particular person in mind.

Materials

LARGE PURSE

Makes one 6 x 8in (15 x 20.5cm) purse

- Lime green suede, at least 10 x 12in (25 x 30.5cm)
- Quilted fuschia satin lining fabric, at least 14in (35cm) square
- 9in (23cm) large-toothed turquoise zipper
- Thread to match suede and satin
- ¾in (18mm)-diameter bell

SMALL PURSE

Makes one 4 x 5 in (10 x 12.5cm) purse

- Red suede, at least 7 x 10in (18 x 25cm)
- Gold satin lining fabric, at least 10in (25cm) square
- 8 x 10in (20.5 x 25cm) batting
- 7in (17.8cm) large-toothed purple zipper
- Thread to match suede and satin
- ½in (12mm)-diameter bell

YOU'LL ALSO NEED:

sewing machine; machine quilting guide; size 8 (60) machine needle; size 12 (80) machine needle; ¼in (6mm) quilter's tape; rotary cutter; quilter's acrylic grid ruler; self-healing cutting mat; hand-sewing needle; zipper foot; and pins.

Instructions

LARGE PURSE

1. *Cut purse lining.* Use rotary cutter to cut 8 x 12in (20.5 x 30.5cm) lining from quilted satin.

2. *Sew zipper to lining.* Lay quilted lining fabric right side up on flat surface. Lay zipper face up along short edge, with pull stop ¼ in (6mm) in from long edge; pin in place. Using zipper foot, stitch ³⁄₁₆in (5mm) from edge (see illustration A, facing page). Match free zipper tape to opposite edge of lining; pin and stitch down in same way (illustration B).

3. *Sew zipper to suede.* Using rotary cutter and cutting mat, cut one 8½ x 12in (21.5 x 30.5cm) rectangle from suede. Lay suede right side up on flat surface. Place zipper right side down along short edge. Using size 12 (80) needle and thread to match suede, stitch through all layers (including lining) ¹⁄₁₆in (1.5mm) in from lining stitching; begin and end stitching even with lining edge (illustration C). Fold suede in half, right sides together, then sew other suede edge to other side of zipper (illustration D). When complete, lining and suede will each straddle zipper.

4. *Sew purse sides.* Open zipper halfway. Lay piece flat, wrong side out, and pin two pairs of suede and lining side edges together. Using appropriate needle and thread, machine-stitch side edges; run stitching on all sides as close to zipper tape as possible; leave 3in (7.5cm) opening along one lining edge for turning (illustration E). Turn purse right side out and slip-stitch opening closed (illustration F). Slip lining down inside purse. Attach bell to zipper pull.

SMALL PURSE

For smaller, unquilted version of Large Purse, cut one 5½ x 8½in (14 x 21.5cm) rectangle from suede and one 5 x 8in (12.5 x 20.5cm) rectangle each from satin lining fabric and batting. Pin satin to batting at corners. Sew the pieces together as for Large Purse, steps 2 through 4. The excess zipper will lodge between the suede and the lining.

designer's tip
* * * * * * *
For a stylish gift, make these purses in two different sizes, but in identical or coordinating colors.

Making the Purses

A. Trim the quilted lining to size. Sew a zipper to one edge.

B. Sew the zipper to the opposite lining edge.

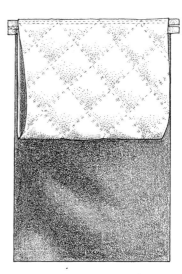

C. Sew one zipper edge to the short edge of a suede rectangle (including the lining).

D. Repeat once more to sew the remaining edges to the other half of the zipper.

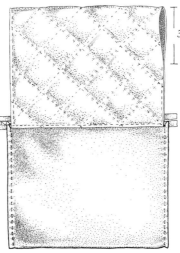

3in

E. Stitch the sides, leaving a 3in (7.5cm) opening in the lining for turning.

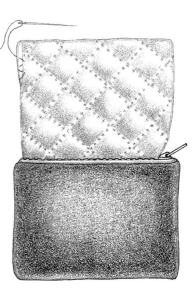

F. Turn the purse right side out, hand-sew the opening, then tuck the lining inside.

Lined Velvet Pouches

Traditionally, any object designed with

a lining—be it a gift bag, a set of drapes, or a jacket—

suggests a certain level of complexity. This

fast and simple technique for making a set of lined gift bags

counters that assumption, however. The basic

configuration resembles a sock. You sew the bag and

lining together, then turn the bag right side out,

then sew the lining closed and slip it inside the bag.

Velvet gives these pouches a deep, plush

texture and "backbone" so that they will stand up on their

own without collapsing. Other full-bodied

fabrics, such as textured damask, heavyweight satin, and

dress-weight woolens would also work.

Materials

Yields five 8 x 7in (20.5 x 18cm) pouches

- ■ *½yd (46cm) 45in (1.2m)-wide velvet*
- ■ *½yd (46cm) 45in (1.2m)-wide acetate lining*
- ■ *Five 27in (68.5cm) drapery tiebacks with tasseled ends*
- ■ *1yd (1m) soutache or similar narrow cord to match velvet*
- ■ *Thread to match velvet and lining*

YOU'LL ALSO NEED:
contrasting thread for basting; sewing machine; scissors; yardstick (meterstick); fabric marking pencil; needle; pins; iron; and ironing board.

OTHER ITEMS, IF NECESSARY:
velvet board or scrap of velvet (for pressing velvet).

Instructions

1. *Iron velvet and cut fabric.* Place velvet face side down on ironing or velvet board and press from wrong side. Measure and mark 18 x 40in (45cm x 101.5cm) rectangle on wrong side of velvet. Then mark 40in (101.5cm) line down center of rectangle to create two 9in (23cm)-wide sections. Pin velvet to lining, right sides together. Cut along marked lines, through both layers, to create two 9 x 40in (23 x 101.5cm) rectangles from each fabric. Mark nap on backside. Remove pins.

2. *Pin and sew velvet and lining.* Pin each velvet rectangle to lining rectangle, right sides together, ⅜in (9mm) from one 40in (101.5cm) edge: Choose same edge on each piece of velvet so nap runs in same direction. Hand-baste two rectangles together using contrasting color thread. Load machine with thread to match velvet and machine-stitch ½in (12mm) from basted edge, removing pins as you go (see illustration A, facing page). Remove basting.

3. *Steam lining.* Place each rectangle lining side up on ironing board. Fold back lining so both lining and velvet face right side up. With iron on lowest steam setting, and holding iron above fabric, steam seam allowance away from velvet.

4. *Form top edge for pouch.* Refold each rectangle wrong sides together so right side of lining faces up and velvet faces ironing board. Make fold in velvet ¼in (6mm) from seam, (illustration B), and finger-press to form top edge. Steam lightly to set crease as in Step 3.

5. *Cut large rectangles into five pouches.* Open both velvet/lining rectangles and lay them flat on work surface. From each rectangle, measure, mark, and cut five 8in (20.5cm)-wide x 17in (43cm)-long rectangles (illustration C).

6. *Cut and sew loops for tasseled cord.* Cut soutache (or substitute) into ten 3½in (9cm) lengths. Fold each length in half, then tie ends in knot 1in (2.5cm) from fold to form loop. Using thread to match velvet, machine-baste two cord loops to sides of velvet rectangle; position loop approximately 2½in (6.5cm) from seam on right side of fabric (illustration D). Repeat to attach all loops.

7. *Assemble pouches.* Lay two rectangles, one with loops and one without, right sides together, edges and seams matching. Machine-baste ½in (12mm) from raw edges across seam for 1in (2.5cm). Pin edges together on all four sides. Starting at point A (illustration E), stitch through both layers ½in (12mm) from edge around three sides, ending at point B. Repeat to stitch four additional pouches.

8. *Add finishing touches.* Clip velvet corners diagonally and clip away excess velvet at seams. Turn pouch right side out, and pick out corners with pin. Fold raw edges of lining ¾in (18mm) to inside, and press with dry iron at lowest setting. Slip-stitch pressed lining edges together using matching thread (illustration F). Poke lining down into pouch. Resteam folded edge at top of pouch as in steps 4 and 5. Slip tasseled tieback through loops, insert gift in pouch, and tie tieback in bow.

designer's tip

✳ ✳ ✳ ✳ ✳ ✳ ✳

Rather than buying off the bolt, first visit the remnants bin, as half a yard (meter) each of fabric and lining is all you need to make five pouches.

Assembling the Pouches

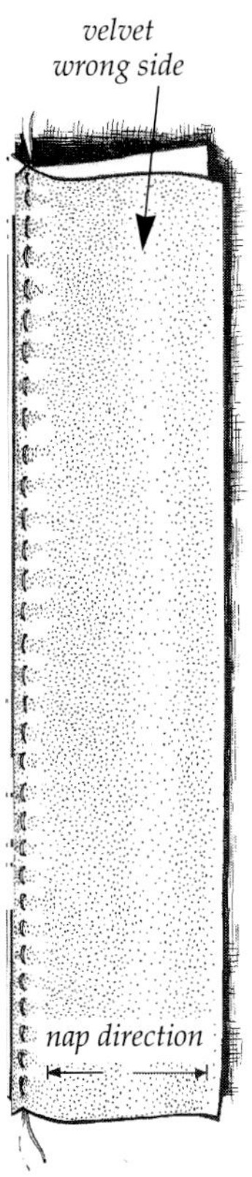

velvet wrong side

velvet right side

lining right side

lining right side

lining right side

nap direction

fold ¼in (6.4mm)

lining right side

velvet right side

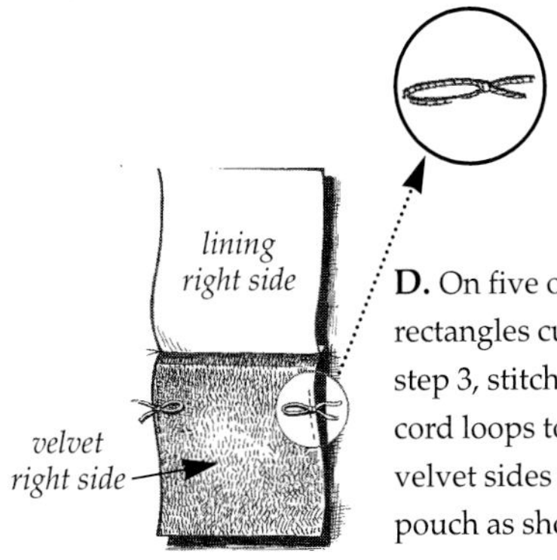

D. On five of the rectangles cut in step 3, stitch two cord loops to the velvet sides of the pouch as shown.

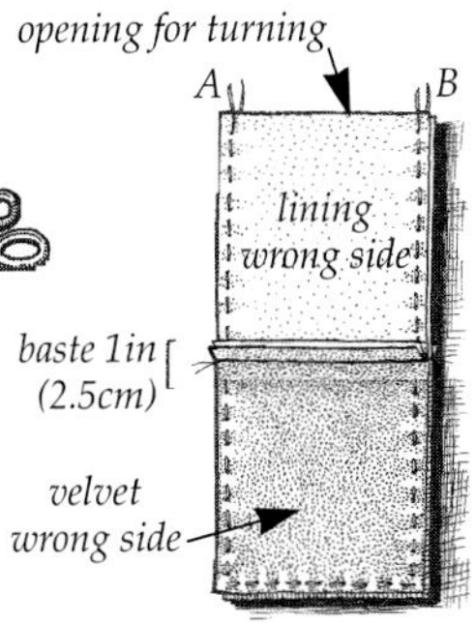

opening for turning

A   B

lining wrong side

baste 1in (2.5cm)

velvet wrong side

E. Lay two rectangles, one with loops and one without, right sides together. Stitch from point A to point B.

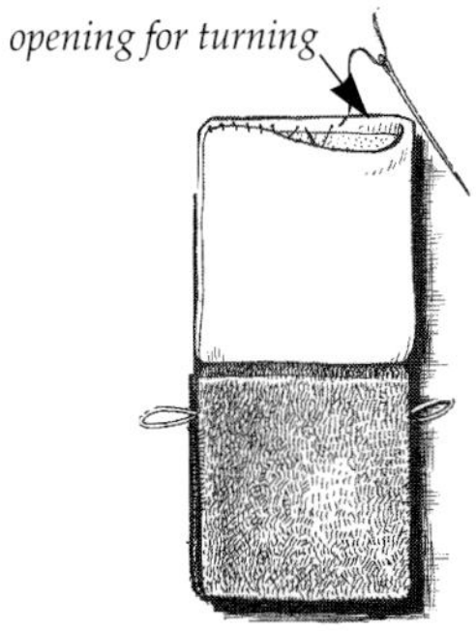

opening for turning

F. Turn each pouch right side out, then fold raw edges of the lining ¾in (18mm) to inside, press, and slip-stitch the edges closed.

A. Stitch each velvet rectangle to its lining rectangle, right sides together, along one 40in (101.5cm) edge.

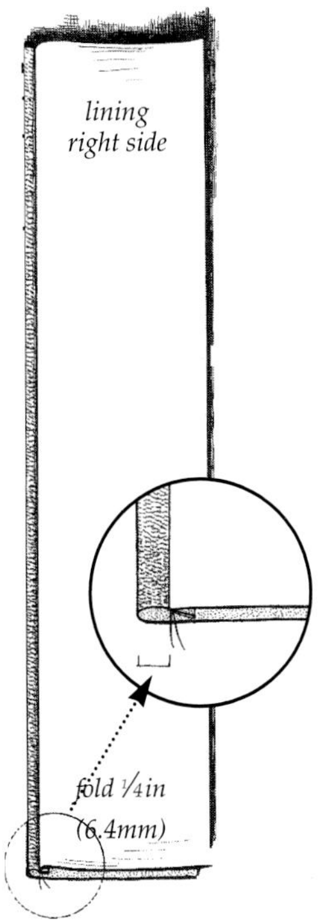

B. Working on ironing board, fold the velvet upward ¼in (6mm) from the seam. First finger-press the velvet, then steam it lightly to form the top edge for the pouch.

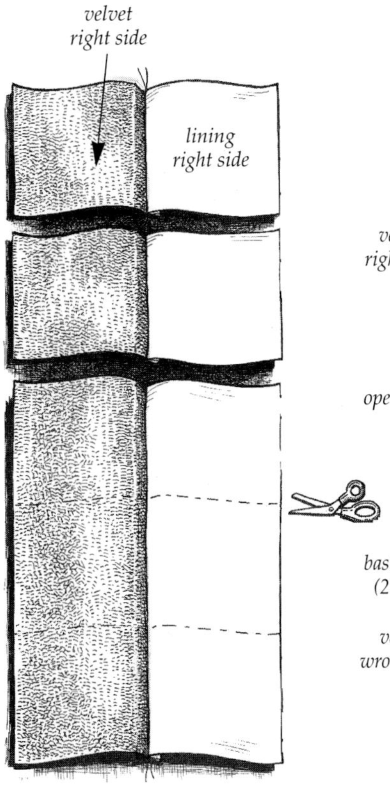

C. Cut the large rectangle into five pouches measuring 8in (20.5cm) wide by 17in (43cm) long.

Faux Brushed-Steel Frame

Although this frame looks like it was

made of brushed steel, in reality it's an ordinary

wooden frame covered with cut aluminum

tooling foil, which can be purchased on a roll

at art supply stores. Bend the foil

around the frame, adhere it to the wood with

heavy-duty spray adhesive, and

create a textured effect of brushed steel

using very fine steel wool.

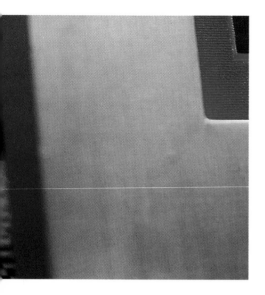

Materials

Yields one frame

- Flat unfinished hardwood frame, with outer dimensions no larger than 8 x 10in (20.5 x 25cm)
- 36-gauge 12in (30.5cm)-wide aluminum tooling foil on roll
- Turquoise velveteen fabric remnant
- One-ply chipboard
- Heavy-duty spray adhesive

YOU'LL ALSO NEED:

hardwood burnishing tool; very fine steel wool; utility knife; self-healing cutting mat; steel ruler; clear acrylic grid ruler; scissors; pencil; newsprint; and masking tape.

---

designer's tip
✳ ✳ ✳ ✳ ✳ ✳ ✳

Use a hardwood frame for this project, not pine. Pine is soft, so it will scratch or dent more easily, which in turn can scratch or dent the tooling foil.

Instructions

1. *Cut foil rectangle.* Cover work surface with newsprint and tape down edges. Unroll 24in (61cm) of foil. Using grid ruler and pencil, mark rectangle 2in (5cm) larger than frame all around. Cut out with scissors.

2. *Cut opening in foil rectangle.* Remove back, glass, and cardboard liner from frame and set aside. Center frame face down on foil rectangle. Holding pencil perpendicular to surface, trace edge of frame opening. (Traced opening will be slightly smaller than actual opening because of pencil position.) Using steel ruler, utility knife, and cutting mat, cut neatly and precisely along marked lines. Discard cut-out section.

3. *Adhere foil strip to opening.* Measure depth and perimeter of frame opening, then add ⅛in (3mm) to perimeter measurement. Mark strip of foil to these dimensions, then cut out as above. Following manufacturer's directions, and working in a well-ventilated space, apply spray adhesive to one side of foil strip. Stand frame on edge, perpendicular to work surface. Set end of strip even with inside corner, adhesive side down, and slowly press onto inside opening, even with wood edges (see illustration A, facing page). When you reach adjacent corner, use burnishing tool to bend foil so it hugs corner angle. Turn frame 90° and repeat process to adhere strip to adjacent edge. Continue all around. When you reach starting point, crimp foil to match angle, cut on crimp line with scissors, and press into place. Burnish entire strip to ensure good adhesion.

4. *Adhere foil to frame front.* Apply spray adhesive to one side of foil cut in step 2. Lay foil adhesive side up. Hold frame face down over foil, make sure openings are centered, and press gently into place. Turn frame foil side up. Press foil onto frame, from opening out to edges, all around. Using burnishing tool, bend foil overlap at edge toward interior (illustration B). Burnish entire surface to flatten foil and insure good adhesion.

5. *Adhere foil to frame edges and back.* Using fingers, bend foil around one edge of frame, then burnish from front to back. Repeat on opposite edge. At each corner of frame, trim excess foil so remainder overlaps just slightly at corner (illustration C). Repeat process on remaining two edges. Bend remaining foil onto back of frame; trim corners on backside diagonally to miter corners (illustration D).

6. *Cut chipboard mat.* Measure length and width of opening at back of frame. Draft rectangle to these dimensions on chipboard. For mat interior opening, draft lines 1in (2.5cm) in from each edge all around; note that about ⅜ (9.5mm) of 1in (2.5cm) mat width will be hidden by recess built into frame opening. Using utility knife, steel ruler, and cutting mat, cut chipboard mat along marked lines.

7. *Laminate velveteen to mat.* From velveteen, cut rectangle ½–1in (1.25–2.5cm) larger than mat all around. Apply spray adhesive to wrong side of fabric and one side of mat. Lay mat adhesive side down on velveteen and press to adhere. Using scissors, poke a hole, then cut an X in interior section. Fold each triangular section onto back of mat, press to adhere, and trim off excess all around (illustration E).

8. *Brush steel surface.* Rub steel wool in circular motion across surface of frame (illustration F) to create brushed-steel appearance.

designer's tip
✷ ✷ ✷ ✷ ✷ ✷ ✷
This aluminum frame features a swirling brushed effect. For variation, use the steel wool to create wavy or straight lines.

Making the Frame

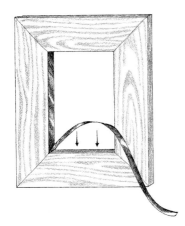

A. Adhere a foil strip to the inside edge of the frame.

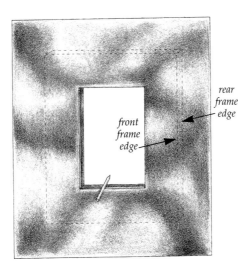

B. Adhere foil to the frame front and burnish down.

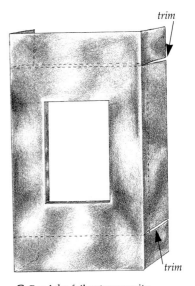

C. Bend the foil onto opposite frame sides, one at a time.

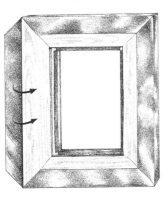

D. Bend and adhere the excess foil to the frame back.

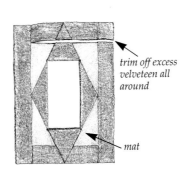

E. Cut a chipboard mat and cover it with velveteen.

F. For a brushed-steel look, rub the foil with fine steel wool.

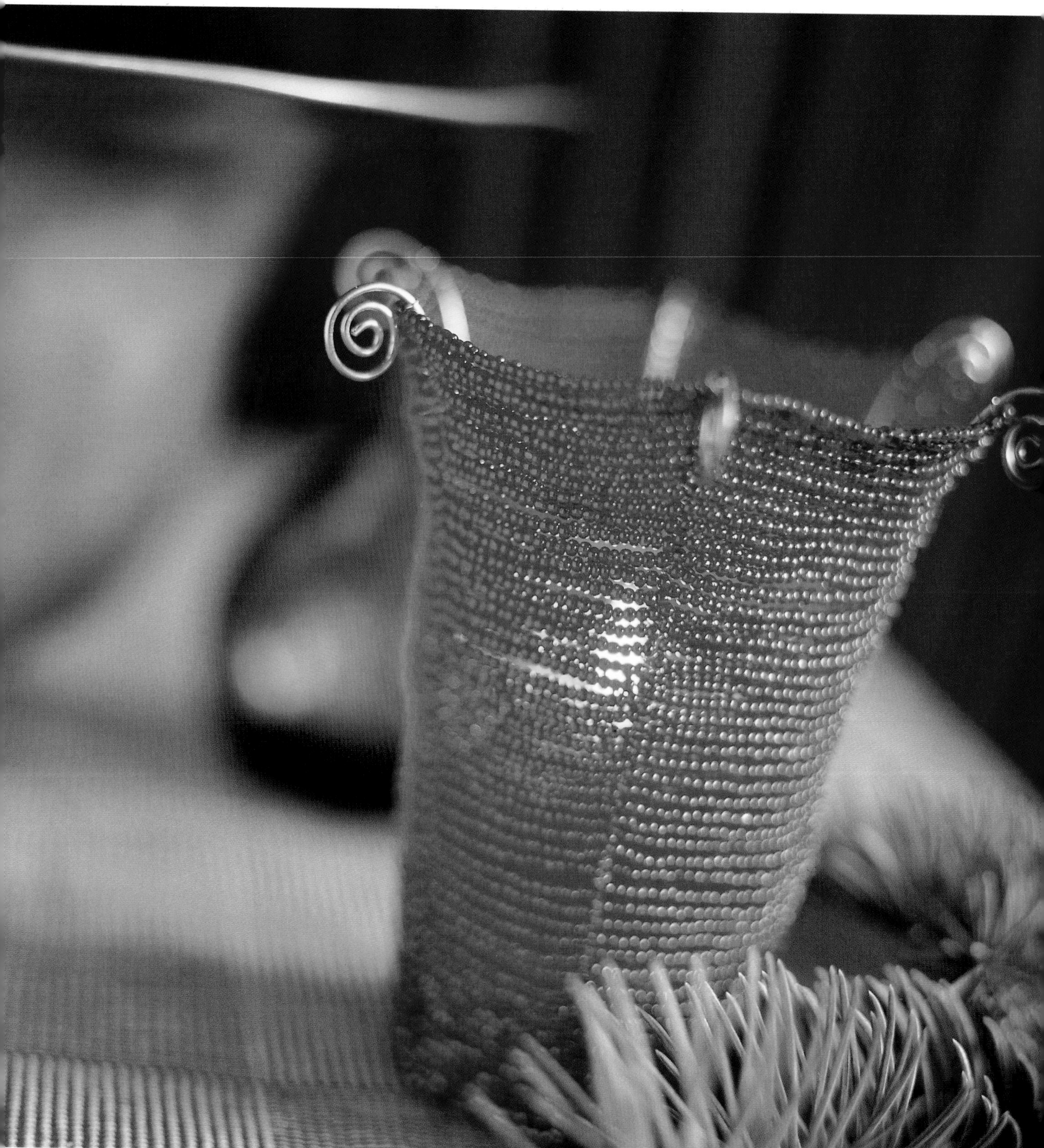

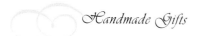

Beaded Votive Candle Holder

This contemporary, colorful candle holder

holds a standard glass votive,

and makes an attractive decoration virtually

anywhere in the house. To make the

candle holder, bend thin brass rods into a curlicue

shape, then string seed beads onto

wire and wrap them around the votive base.

To facilitate beading, be sure to

purchase seed beads that are prestrung on thread.

Materials

Yields one beaded votive candle holder

- Standard glass votive (approximately 1⅞in [4.7cm] in diameter x 2⅝in [6.7cm] tall)
- Twenty 20in (51cm) strands silver-lined glass seed beads
- Two 36in (1m)-long x .045in (1.1mm)-diameter brass rods
- 28-gauge brass spool wire
- 24-gauge brass spool wire

YOU'LL ALSO NEED:

round-nose pliers; flat-nose pliers; chain-nose pliers; wire cutters; flexible tape measure; permanent marking pen; flannel cloth or corrugated cardboard, top ply removed; masking tape; and narrow-necked bottle.

designer's tip
✳ ✳ ✳ ✳ ✳ ✳ ✳

The easiest way to slide seed beads from their thread onto wire is to move a few inches (cm) of beading at a time. If the wire is straight, you can push it through the bead holes along the thread path. After you have wired a short section, remove the thread from it.

Instructions

1. *Transfer beads to wire.* Set aside one 20in (51cm) strand of seed beads. Lay remaining nineteen strands on flannel cloth or in corrugated cardboard channels. Carefully transfer beads to 28-gauge spool wire a few inches (cm) at a time; do not cut wire from spool. Continue until you have transferred five strands (100in [250cm]). Clip wire to measure 150in (375cm) total; bend wire at each end into loop to prevent beads from sliding off. Repeat process to make four wire strands (final strand will have 80in [200cm], not 100in [250cm], of beads).

2. *Bend and shape brass rods.* Cut 16in (41cm) length of brass rod. Mark midpoint with permanent pen. Measure from midpoint 1in (2.5cm) in each direction, and make two additional marks. Using flat-nose pliers, grip rod at outer point and bend up at right angle; make bend at second outer point in same way (see illustration A, facing page). Cut and bend two more rods to match. Grip one rod between thumb and forefinger about 1in (2.5cm) beyond bend. Using short, deliberate motions, bend rod into gentle outward curve. Using round-nose pliers, coil end into loop. Grip loop with flat-nose pliers, and continue bending to form flat, open coil; for even spacing, move pliers along rod in ¼in (6mm) increments, bending as you go. Repeat process to shape other side. Shape two remaining rods to match.

3. *Join brass rods.* Rest votive upside down on bottle neck. Lay one rod across votive base, so coiled ends hang down sides. Using round-nose pliers, bend two remaining rods at midpoint to make 60° angle (illustration A, facing page). Set angled rods alongside first rod, midpoints touching, to form six-spoke design. Bind rods together at midpoints with 24-gauge wire. Measure and mark votive circumference into six equal segments. Align each spoke with mark. Pull rods approximately 1/16in (1.6mm) off glass votive (to allow room for slipping 28-gauge wire between rod and glass), then tape in place (illustration B).

4. *Bead base of votive.* Cut 26in (66cm) length of 28-gauge wire. Twist end three times around brass spoke at hub. String two beads from reserved strand onto wire, slide beads snug against spoke, and twist wire once tightly around adjacent spoke. Repeat process to complete circle of beads around hub. For next round, string three beads between spokes. Make beads as snug as possible, and allow a bead to sit on top of each spoke to conceal it (illustration C). Continue in this manner, increasing bead count between spokes on each round, until all reserved beads are used. To end off, spiral wire along spoke between beads for several rounds, pulling snug after each wrap with chain-nose pliers; clip excess and crimp end against inside spoke.

5. *Complete beading.* Join on one strand of prestrung beads, twisting wire end tightly around spoke. Carry strand across frame to next spoke, separate beads to expose wire, then wrap wire once around spoke, pulling snug with chain-nose pliers. Strive for even tension; strand spanning spokes should be snug, but not tight, and should not sag. Test-fit votive holder. After beading base and about one-quarter of sides, remove tape and glass votive and stand project upright (illustration D). Continue beading up sides until you reach coiled spirals.

designer's tip
✶ ✶ ✶ ✶ ✶ ✶ ✶

Use the three types of pliers recommended for this project for the best result, as each performs a specific function that will make the process go smoothly. Generally, chain-nose pliers are meant to open and close crimps. Round-nose pliers are ideal for bending round wire. Flat-nose pliers enable you to hold flat or square objects firmly.

Making the Candle Holder

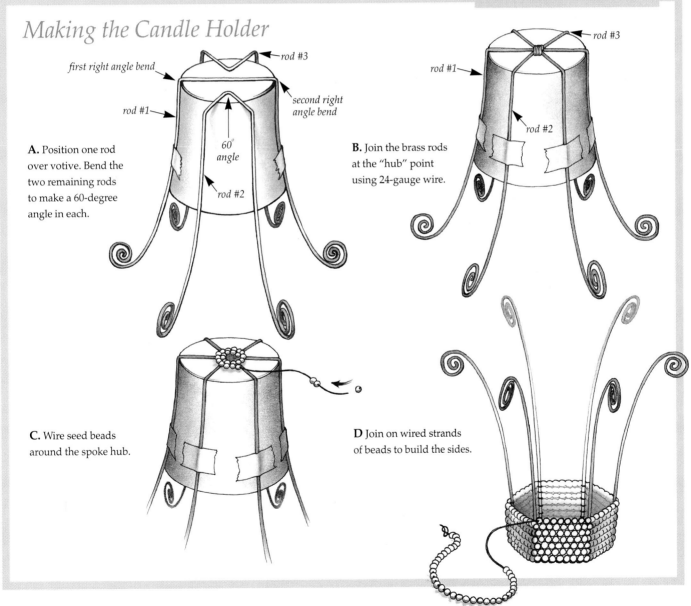

first right angle bend

rod #3

rod #1

second right angle bend

60° *angle*

rod #2

A. Position one rod over votive. Bend the two remaining rods to make a 60-degree angle in each.

rod #3

rod #1

rod #2

B. Join the brass rods at the "hub" point using 24-gauge wire.

C. Wire seed beads around the spoke hub.

D Join on wired strands of beads to build the sides.

Custom-Fit
Teddy Bear Sweaters

Knitting sweaters for teddy bears seems

an easy endeavor on one hand, as the garments are small,

but daunting on the other, in terms of

figuring out the measurements. You can master the process,

however, with five quick measurements and a

series of simple calculations. Start by measuring the bear,

then use those measurements to calculate

the specific stitch and inch (centimeter) amounts required.

Materials

FOR BOTH SWEATERS

- 1.75oz (50g) ball red worsted or bulky weight yarn for red sweater*
- Two 1.75oz balls (50g) worsted or bulky weight yarn, one each in green and white, for striped sweater*
- Teddy bear
- * Additional yarn may be necessary for larger bears.

YOU'LL ALSO NEED:

knitting needles U.S. size 8/Canadian size 6 (5mm) or size required to obtain gauge; straight and double-pointed knitting needles U.S. size 6/Canadian size 8 (4.25 mm) or two sizes smaller than gauge size; tape measure; ruler; pencil; calculator; pins; stitch markers; scissors; and tapestry needle.

---

designer's tip
✳ ✳ ✳ ✳ ✳ ✳ ✳
Use the sweaters to personalize a teddy bear gift or to turn a collection of bears into a decorative Christmas display.

Instructions

RED SWEATER

Note: Knit test swatch and check gauge before you begin.

1. Create custom schematic. See box, facing page.

2. Knit back and front. Referring to schematic and using smaller needles and red yarn, cast on **(a)** sts for back. Work in k1, p1 ribbing for ½in (12mm) (or desired depth); end wrong side. Change to larger needles. Work in ss until piece measures **(b)** inches (cm) from ribbing edge; end wrong side. Bind off loosely. Work front same as back.

3. Join back to front. Using tapestry needle and yarn, sew back to front for **(d)** sts at each shoulder. Mark back and front armhole edges **(g)** inches (cm) from bottom edge.

4. Knit sleeves. From right side, with larger needles, pick up **(e)** sts evenly spaced between armhole markers. Work in ss for **(h)** inches minus ½in (12mm) (or ribbing depth established in step 2); end wrong side. Change to smaller needles and work in k1, p1 ribbing for ½in (12mm) (or established ribbing depth). Bind off. Work second sleeve to match on opposite side.

5. Knit neck ribbing. With dp needles, pick up **(c)** sts evenly around neck edge. Work k1, p1 ribbing in round for ½in (12mm). Bind off loosely.

6. Sew side and sleeve seams. Using tapestry needle and yarn and with right sides together, backstitch arm and side seams on one side. Repeat to join opposite side.

STRIPED SWEATER

Note: Knit test swatch and check gauge before you begin.

1. Create custom schematic. See box, facing page.

2. Knit back and front. Referring to schematic and using smaller needles and green yarn, cast on **(a)** sts for back. Work in k1, p1 ribbing for ½in (12mm) (or desired depth); end wrong side. Change to larger needles and white yarn. Work two rows ss in white yarn, two in green yarn, continuing until entire piece measures **(b)** from ribbing edge; end wrong side. Bind off loosely. Work front same as back.

3. Join back to front. See Red Sweater, step 3.

4. Knit sleeves. From right side, with larger needles and white yarn, pick up **(e)** sts evenly spaced between armhole markers. Work two rows ss in white yarn, two in green yarn, continuing until piece measures approximately **(h)** minus ½in (12mm) (or ribbing depth established in step 2); end wrong side white row. Change to smaller needles and green yarn and work in k1, p1 ribbing for ½in (12mm) (or established ribbing depth). Bind off. Work second sleeve to match on opposite side.

5. *Knit neck ribbing.* With dp needles and white yarn, pick up **(c)** sts evenly around neck edge. Work k1, p1 ribbing in round for ½in (12mm) (or established ribbing depth). Bind off loosely.

6. *Sew side and sleeve seams.* See Red Sweater, step 6.

> **To convert inches to stitches, multiply inches by 4. To convert stitches to inches, divide by 4.**
> **Gauge**
> (calculated on larger needles)
> 4 stitches = 1 in (2.5cm)
> 6 rows = 1 in (2.5cm)
> **Key**
> dp = double-pointed
> p = pearl
> k = knit
> ss = stockinette stitch
> st = stitch
> sts = stitches

Creating a Custom Schematic

For each item **(a)** through **(h)**, measure bear and make calculations as directed. Photocopy or draw schematic below, then record results in appropriate spots **(a)** through **(h)**. Note that **(a)**, **(c)**, **(d)**, and **(e)** should be expressed as sts, and **(b)**, **(f)**, **(g)**, and **(h)** as inches (cm).

■ **(a)** Back and front widths: Measure around bear hips at widest part, add 1in (2.5cm) Divide by 2. Multiply by 4 (stitch gauge) to achieve number of sts.

■ **(b)** Total length: Measure bear from shoulder to crotch.

■ **(c)** Neck: Measure around neck of bear, add ½in (12mm). Multiply by 4 to achieve number of sts.

■ **(d)** Shoulders: Divide total neck sts **(c)** by 2. Subtract from total back sts **(a)**. Divide by 2 to achieve number of sts for each shoulder.

■ **(e)** Wrist: Measure around bear wrist, add 1in (2.5cm). Multiply by 4 to achieve number of sts.

■ **(f)** Back (or front) armhole: Divide wrist sts **(e)** by 2, then multiply by 6 to achieve armhole length in inches.

■ **(g)** Length of front (or back) to armhole: Subtract armhole length **(f)** from total length **(b)**.

■ **(h)** Sleeve length: Measure bear's arm from shoulder to wrist.

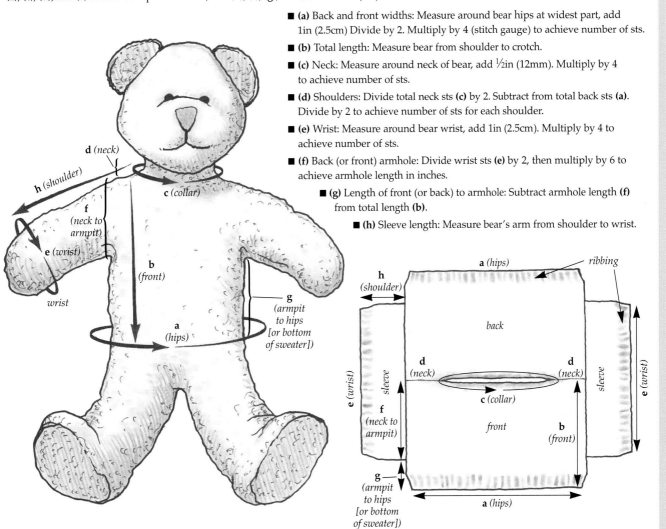

Terry Cloth Bunny and Piglet

You can delight every child on your gift list

this year with a handmade stuffed

bunny or piglet sewn from terry cloth. The animals

are filled with plastic pellets and fiberfill,

giving them an appealing roundness and making

them poseable. To add personality, you'll

need a few pom-pons and a series of simple

embroidery stitches.

Materials

BUNNY
- *12 x 12in (30.5 x 30.5cm) white terry cloth*
- *2 x 12in (5 x 30.5cm) pink terry cloth*
- *Matching sewing thread*
- *1½in (3.8cm) white pom-pom*
- *Two ¼in (6mm) black pom-poms*
- *Brown and white embroidery thread*
- *Plastic pellets*
- *Fiberfill*
- *Washable fabric glue*

PIGLET
- *12 x 12in (30.5 x 30.5cm) pink terry cloth*
- *2 x 12in (5 x 30.5cm) cream terry cloth*
- *Matching sewing thread*
- *Two ¼in (6mm) black pom-poms*
- *Brown and pink embroidery thread*
- *Plastic pellets*
- *Fiberfill*
- *Washable fabric glue*

YOU'LL ALSO NEED:
bunny and piglet patterns (see page 187); sewing machine; sewing shears; ball-head pins; long hand-sewing needle; embroidery needle; size 3 (3mm) steel crochet hook; fabric pen; and access to photocopier with enlarger.

Instructions
BUNNY
Note: Sew all pieces making scant ¼in (6mm) seams.

1. *Cut terry cloth pieces.* Prepare bunny patterns (see page 187). From white terry cloth, cut one 2in (5cm)-wide strip along lengthwise grain; set aside for ears. Using patterns, cut one body front, one body back, two arms, two head fronts, and two head backs.

2. *Make ears.* Stack pink and white terry cloth strips wrong sides together; pin ear pattern to them. Straight-stitch along pattern outline through both layers. Reposition pattern and stitch second ear in same way. Cut out ears close to stitching. Place one ear on machine bed pink side up. Using pink upper thread and white bobbin thread, satin-stitch curved edge all around. Finish second ear in same way.

3. *Stitch head.* Fold short edge of ear pink side in, and machine-baste to head front between marks. Pin one pair head front and back right sides together; stitch seam, leaving neck edge open (see illustration A, facing page). Repeat to join second pair of head pieces. Sew both halves together to complete head, then turn head right side out (illustration B).

4. *Stitch body.* Fold body back in half right side in; stitch center back seam, leaving opening for turning. Stitch arms to body front, right sides together, making raglan-style seams. Sew body front to body back, easing fit all around; leave neck edge open. Do not turn (illustration C).

5. *Join head to body.* Slip head inside body, right sides together and seams matching. Stitch neck seam all around. Turn body right side out through back opening. Stuff head firmly with fiberfill to fill out curves and muzzle. Pad chest and arms lightly with fiberfill. Fill tummy cavity and legs with approximately ½ cup (125ml) plastic pellets. Slip-stitch opening closed (illustration D).

6. *Add tail and facial details.* Using white thread, hand-tack white pom-pom to back rump for tail. Insert two ball-head pins into head to fix position for eyes; mark with fabric pen and remove pins. Knot end of white thread. Insert needle into back neck and draw out at one eye mark; pull snug so knot pulls through terry cloth and lodges inside fiberfill. Reinsert needle into head at mark, draw out at back neck, and pull gently to indent eye socket. Repeat to make second eye socket; end off. Using six strands brown thread, embroider nose in satin stitch and muzzle in straight stitch; using white thread, make two straight stitches at end of each limb to suggest paw pads. Glue two black pom-poms to eye sockets; let dry overnight (illustration E).

Making the Bunny

A. Sew the front and back heads together, catching an ear in the seam.

B. Join the two head halves and turn right side out.

C. Join the front and back bodies, easing the seams to fit.

D. Join the head and body, turn, and stuff from the back.

E. Add facial features using pom-poms and embroidery thread.

PIGLET

Note: Sew all pieces making scant ¼in (6mm) seams.

1. *Cut terry cloth pieces.* Prepare piglet patterns (see page 187). From pink terry cloth, cut one 2in (5cm)-wide x 6in (15cm)-long strip along lengthwise grain; set aside for ears. Using patterns, cut one body front, one body back, two arms, two head fronts, and two head backs. From cream terry cloth strip, cut one 6in (15cm)-long strip for ears and five snout/foot circles.

2. *Make ears.* Follow Bunny, step 2.

designer's tips
✳ ✳ ✳ ✳ ✳ ✳ ✳
You can use any fabric with a rough texture for this project, including terry bouclé, recycled terry towels, or stretch terry.

designer's tips

✳ ✳ ✳ ✳ ✳ ✳ ✳

ADAPTING THIS PATTERN
The basic body patterns used for the bunny and piglet can be adapted to create other creatures. You can adapt the ear patterns for a new animal—shorter bunny ears, for example, could work for a puppy—or draw new patterns in shapes as simple as those provided here. You can also make a variety of tails by braiding or crocheting embroidery thread.

✳ ✳ ✳ ✳ ✳ ✳ ✳

Create a coordinated menagerie by using fabric scraps from one toy's body for the trims of another.

3. *Stitch head.* Place ear cream side down on head front between marks; machine-baste in place. Pin one pair head front and back right sides together; stitch seam, leaving neck edge open. Repeat to join second pair of head pieces. Sew both halves together, leaving straight edge open for snout. Ease snout into opening, right sides together, and stitch by hand or machine (illustration F). Turn head right side out.

4. *Stitch body.* Using double thickness (twelve strands) pink embroidery thread and size 3 (3mm) steel crochet hook, chain fifty. To create curly tail, single-crochet (double-crochet, in Canada) in every other chain back to starting point; end off. Fold body back in half right side in, sandwiching end of tail in center back seam. Stitch seam, leaving opening for turning. Stitch arms to body front, right sides together, making raglan-style seams. Sew body front to body back, easing fit all around; leave marked area shown on pattern open. Ease foot into each opening, right sides together, and stitch as for snout. Do not turn (illustration G).

5. *Join head to body.* Follow Bunny, step 5.

6. *Add facial details.* Indent eye sockets as for Bunny, step 6. Thread embroidery needle with six strands of brown thread; embroider nostrils and mouth in straight stitch. Glue two black pom-poms to eye sockets; let dry overnight (illustration H).

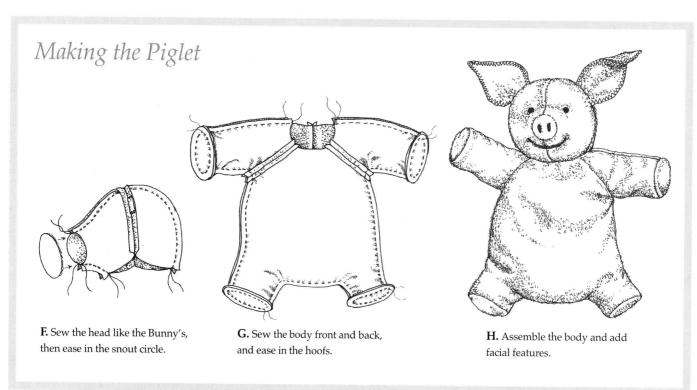

Making the Piglet

F. Sew the head like the Bunny's, then ease in the snout circle.

G. Sew the body front and back, and ease in the hoofs.

H. Assemble the body and add facial features.

Patterns

Embossed Tree Ornaments

(see page 38)

[photocopy all pieces at 100%]

SMALL STAR CUTTING DIAGRAM

½in (1.3cm)

| 1in (2.5cm) | 1in (2.5cm) | 1in (2.5cm) | 1in (2.5cm) | 1in (2.5cm) | 1in (2.5cm) |
| 1in (2.5cm) | 1in (2.5cm) | 1in (2.5cm) | 1in (2.5cm) | 1in (2.5cm) | 1in (2.5cm) |

2¼in (5.7cm)

½in (1.3cm)

Moravian Glitter Stars

(see page 58) [photocopy both pieces at 200%]

LARGE STAR CUTTING DIAGRAM

1in (2.5cm)

waste

| 2in (5.1cm) | 2in (5.1cm) | 2in (5.1cm) | 2in (5.1cm) | 2in (5.1cm) | 2in (5.1cm) |
| 2in (5.1cm) | 2in (5.1cm) | 2in (5.1cm) | 2in (5.1cm) | 2in (5.1cm) | 2in (5.1cm) | 1in (2.5cm) |

4½in (11.4cm)

waste

Appliquéd Wool Stocking
(see page 78)

stitching line

STOCKING
(cut two)

[photocopy at 200%]

leave top open

CUFF
(cut two from wool and two from lining)

[photocopy at 200%]

cutting line

stitching line

sew hanging loop here

STOCKING BERRIES
[photocopy at 100%]

(cut one)

(cut three)

CUFF LEAVES
[photocopy at 100%]

(cut one)

(cut one)

Gilded Glitter Village *(see page 88)*
[photocopy all pieces at 200%]

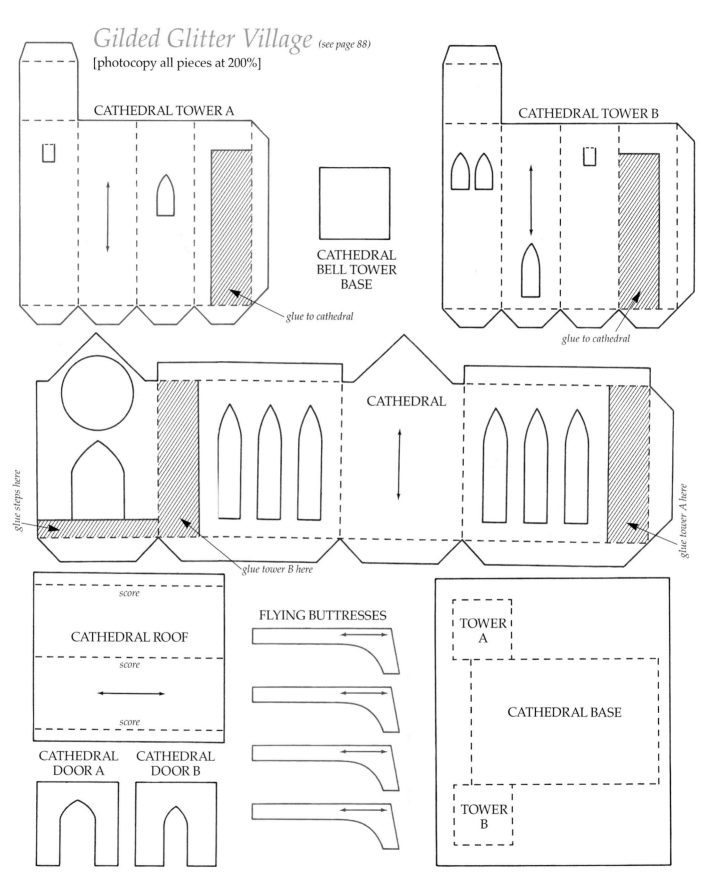

CATHEDRAL TOWER A

CATHEDRAL TOWER B

glue to cathedral

CATHEDRAL
BELL TOWER
BASE

glue to cathedral

CATHEDRAL

glue steps here

glue tower B here

glue tower A here

score

CATHEDRAL ROOF

score

score

FLYING BUTTRESSES

TOWER
A

CATHEDRAL BASE

CATHEDRAL
DOOR A

CATHEDRAL
DOOR B

TOWER
B

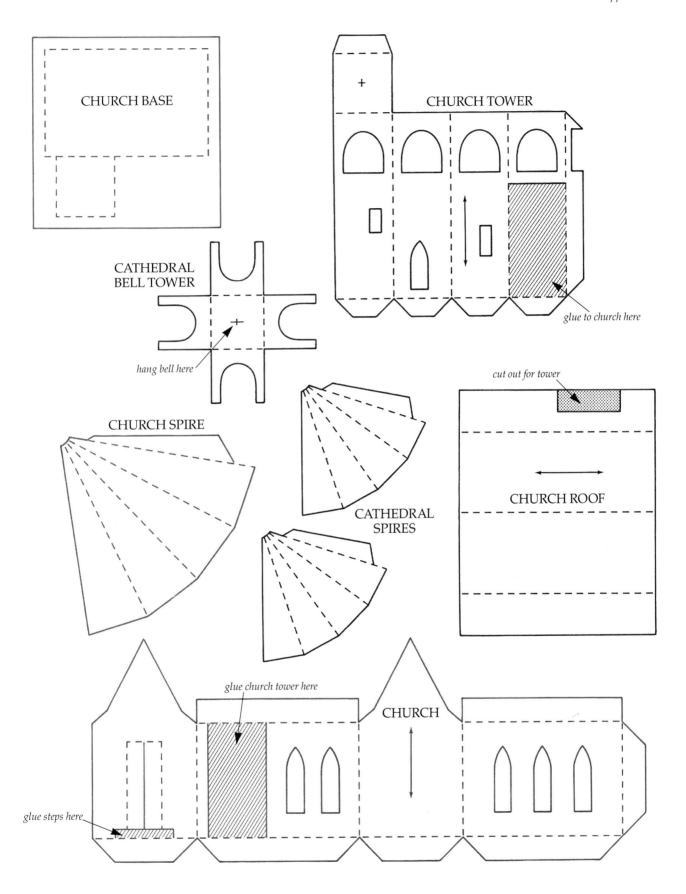

CHURCH BASE

CHURCH TOWER

CATHEDRAL
BELL TOWER

glue to church here

hang bell here

cut out for tower

CHURCH SPIRE

CATHEDRAL
SPIRES

CHURCH ROOF

glue church tower here

CHURCH

glue steps here

Gilded Glitter Village *(see page 88)*

[photocopy all pieces at 200%]

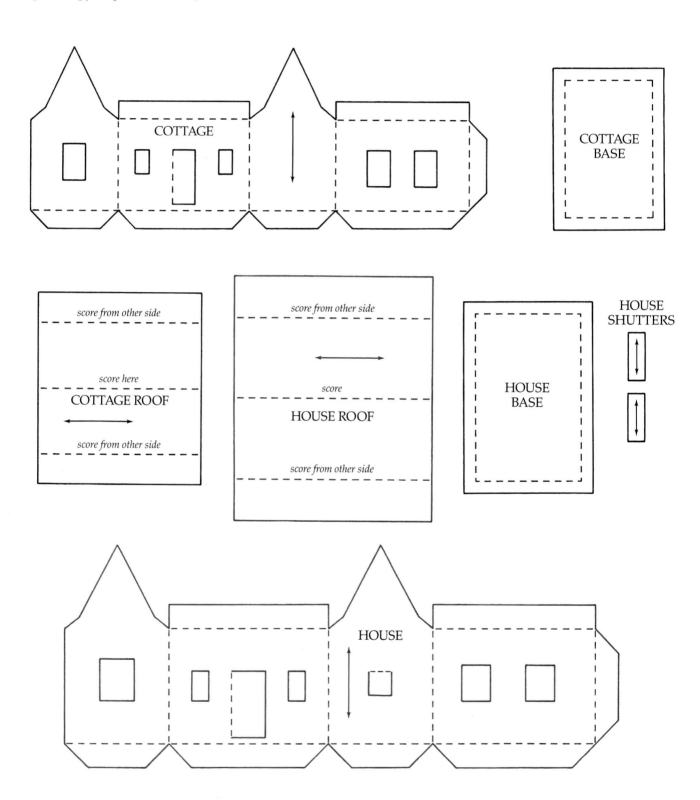

Court Jester Stocking (see page 104) [photocopy all pieces at 200%]

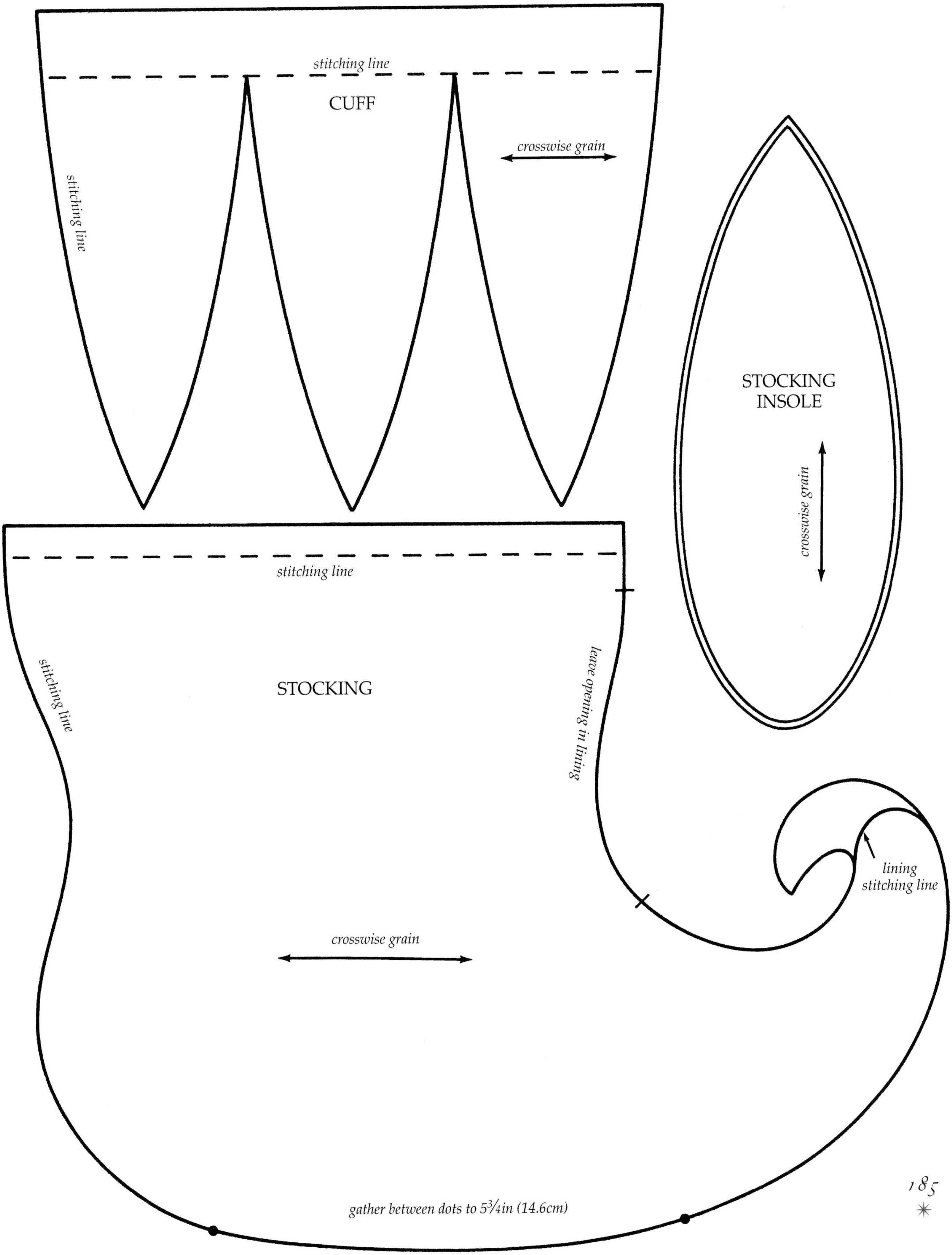
stitching line
CUFF
crosswise grain
stitching line
STOCKING
INSOLE
crosswise grain
stitching line
STOCKING
stitching line
leave opening in lining
lining
stitching line
crosswise grain
gather between dots to 5¾in (14.6cm)

Cuffed Velvet Stocking
(see page 84)

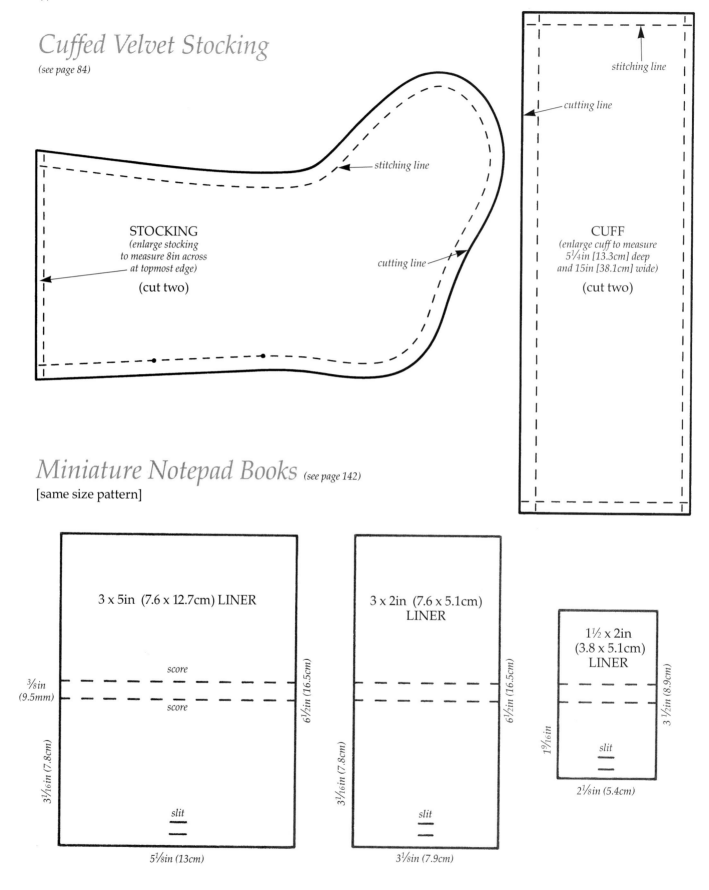

STOCKING
*(enlarge stocking
to measure 8in across
at topmost edge)*

(cut two)

stitching line

cutting line

stitching line

cutting line

CUFF
*(enlarge cuff to measure
5¼in [13.3cm] deep
and 15in [38.1cm] wide)*

(cut two)

Miniature Notepad Books (see page 142)

[same size pattern]

3 x 5in (7.6 x 12.7cm) LINER

score

score

³⁄₈in
(9.5mm)

6½in (16.5cm)

3¹⁄₁₆in (7.8cm)

slit

5⅛in (13cm)

3 x 2in (7.6 x 5.1cm)
LINER

6½in (16.5cm)

3¹⁄₁₆in (7.8cm)

slit

3⅛in (7.9cm)

1½ x 2in
(3.8 x 5.1cm)
LINER

3½in (8.9cm)

1⁹⁄₁₆in

slit

2⅛in (5.4cm)

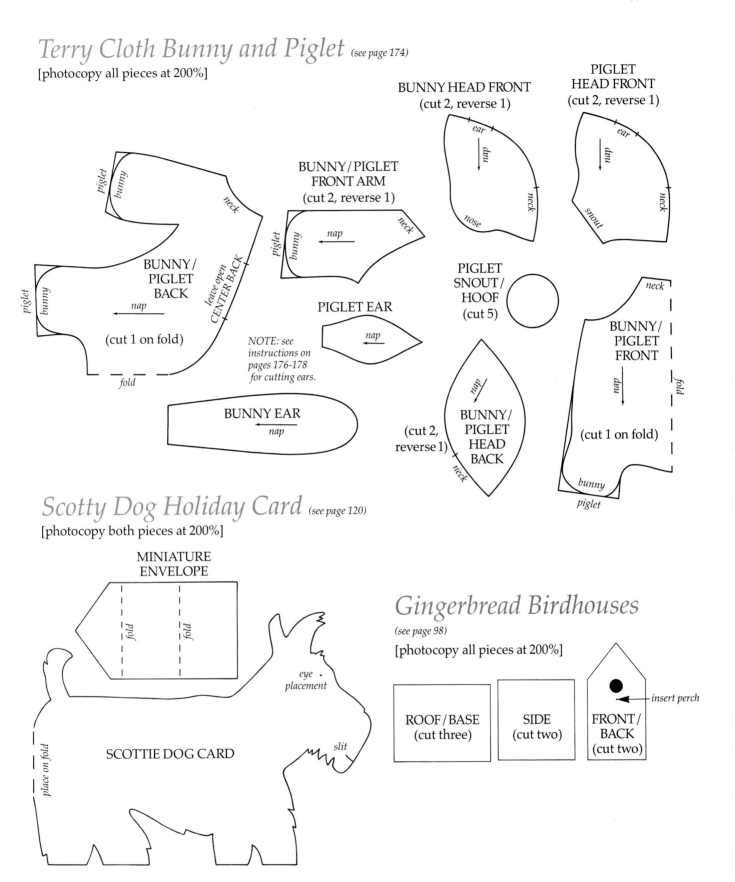

Terry Cloth Bunny and Piglet *(see page 174)*
[photocopy all pieces at 200%]

BUNNY HEAD FRONT (cut 2, reverse 1)

PIGLET HEAD FRONT (cut 2, reverse 1)

ear *nap* *neck* *nose*

ear *nap* *neck* *snout*

BUNNY/PIGLET FRONT ARM (cut 2, reverse 1)

piglet *bunny* *nap* *neck*

BUNNY/PIGLET BACK

piglet *bunny* *neck* *leave open CENTER BACK* *nap* *fold*

(cut 1 on fold)

piglet *bunny*

PIGLET EAR

nap

NOTE: see instructions on pages 176-178 for cutting ears.

BUNNY EAR *nap*

PIGLET SNOUT/HOOF (cut 5)

nap

(cut 2, reverse 1)

BUNNY/PIGLET HEAD BACK *neck*

BUNNY/PIGLET FRONT

neck *nap* *fold*

(cut 1 on fold)

bunny *piglet*

Scotty Dog Holiday Card *(see page 120)*
[photocopy both pieces at 200%]

MINIATURE ENVELOPE

fold *fold*

eye placement

slit

SCOTTIE DOG CARD

place on fold

Gingerbread Birdhouses
(see page 98)

[photocopy all pieces at 200%]

ROOF/BASE (cut three)

SIDE (cut two)

FRONT/BACK (cut two)

insert perch

$\mathcal{S}ources$

Contact each firm individually for the latest price list or catalog.

Art Supplies

Above Ground Art Supplies
71 McCaul
Toronto, ON M5T 2X1
416-591-1601

Daniel Smith
4150 First Avenue South
P.O. Box 84268
Seattle, WA 98124-5568
800-426-6740

Delta Art and Drafting Supply
12506 118 Avenue
Edmonton, AB T5L 2K6
403-455-7983

Dick Blick Art Materials
P.O. Box 1267
Galesburg, IL 61402-1267
800-447-8192

Janovic Plaza's Incomplete Catalogue for Decorative and Scenic Painters
30-35 Thomson Avenue
Long Island City, NY 11101
800-772-4381

New York Central Art Supply, Inc.
62 Third Avenue
New York, NY 10003
800-950-6111

Omer DeSerres
1763 St-Denis
Montreal, QC H2X 3K4
514-284-2911

Pearl Paint Company, Inc.
308 Canal Street
New York, NY 10013-2572
800-221-6845 x2297

Candle Making

Alberta Beeswax and Candlemaking Supplies
10611 170 Street
Edmonton, AB T5P 4WZ
403-413-0350

Barker Candle Supplies
15106 10th Avenue S.W.
Seattle, WA 98166
800-543-0601

Pourette Candle Making Supplies
1418 N.W. 53rd Street
P.O. Box 17056
Seattle, WA 98107
800-888-9425

Walnut Hill
Green Lane and Wilson Avenue
P.O. Box 599
Bristol, PA 19007
800-NEEDWAX

Decorative Baking Goods

King Arthur Flour Baker's Catalogue
P.O. Box 876
Norwich, VT 05055-0876
800-827-6836

Sweet Celebrations, Inc.
7009 Washington Avenue South
Edina, MN 55439
800-328-6722

Floral/Herbal Supplies

A World of Plenty
P.O. Box 1153
Hermantown, MN 55810-9724
218-729-6761

Richters
Goodwood, ON L0C 1A0
905-640-6677

San Francisco Herb Co.
250 14th Street
San Francisco, CA 94103
800-227-4530

General Craft Supplies

Craft King
P.O. Box 90637
Lakeland, FL 33804
800-769-9494

LewisCraft
477 Paul Street
Moncton, NB E1A 5R4
506-857-9585

Loomis and Toles
1546 Barrington
Halifax, NS B3J 1Z3
800-565-1545

Nasco Arts & Crafts
901 Janesville Avenue
P.O. Box 901
Fort Atkinson, WI 53538-0901
800-558-9595

National Artcraft Co.
7996 Darrow Road
Twinsburg, OH 44087
800-793-0152

Sax Arts & Crafts
P.O. Box 51710
New Berlin, WI 53151
800-326-7555

Sunshine Discount Crafts
P.O. Box 301
Largo, FL 34649-0301
800-729-2878

Paper Arts and Stamps

Au Papier Japonais
24 Fairmount W
Montreal, QC H2T 2M1
514-276-6863

Charrette
P.O. Box 4010
Woburn, MA 01888-4010
800-367-3729

Fascinating Folds
P.O. Box 10070
Glendale, AZ 85318
800-968-2418

Good Stamps—Stamp Goods
30901 Timberline Road
Willits, CA 95490
800-637-6401

Maine Street Stamps
P.O. Box 14
Kingfield, ME 04947
207-265-2500

Sewing and Fabric Supplies

Atlanta Thread and Supply Co.
695 Red Oak Road
Stockbridge, GA 30281
800-847-1001

Clotilde, Inc.
2 Sew Smart Way
Stevens Point, WI 54481-8031
800-772-2891

Dressmaker's
2186 St. Catherine W
Montreal, QC H3M 1M7
514-935-7421

The Fabric Cottage
16 Crowfoot Terrace NW
Calgary, AB T3G 4J8
403-241-3070

M & J Trimming Co.
1008 Sixth Avenue
New York, NY 10018
212-391-9072

Nancy's Notions Ltd.
P.O. Box 683
Beaver Dam, WI 53916-0683
800-833-0690

Newark Dressmaker Supply
6473 Ruch Road
P.O. Box 20730
Lehigh Valley, PA 18002-0730
800-736-6783

Specialty Craft Supplies

Alpine Imports
7104 N. Alpine Road
Rockford, IL 61111
800-654-6114

The Beadcraft Store
130 Davis Drive
Newmarket, ON L3Y 2M1
905-853-6083

The Beadloom
1146-4700 Kingsway
Burnaby, BC V5H 4M1
514-486-6425

Bead Emporium of Montreal
368 Victoria
Westmount, QC H32 2N4
514-486-6425

Beadworks, Inc.
149 Water Street
Norwalk, CT 06854
203-852-9108

Metalliferous
34 West 46th Street
New York, NY 10036
212-944-0909

Tinker Bob's Tinware
209 Summit Street
Norwich, CT 06360
860-886-7365

Viking Woodcrafts, Inc.
1317 8th Street S.E.
Waseca, MN 56093
800-328-0116

Walnut Hollow
1409 State Road 23
Dept. CS
Dodgeville, WI 53533
800-950-5101

Credits

Illustration:

HARRY DAVIS:
Wiring a Pine Cone Invisibly

MICHAEL GELLATLY:
Della Robbia Wreath
Evergreen, Rose, and Lime Wreath
Glitter Balls
Moravian Glitter Stars
Gilded Glitter Village
Gilded Candles
Scotty Dog Holiday Card
Laminated Greeting Cards
Rubber Stamp Gift Tags
Miniature Notepad Books
Pavé Box
Beaded Votive Candle Holder
Custom-Fit Teddy Bear Sweaters

JUDY LOVE:
Empire-Style Door Wreath
Appliquéd Wool Stocking
Stationery Greeting Cards
Terry Cloth Bunny and Piglet

NENAD JAKESEVIC:
White Rose Wreath
Trio of Glass Balls
Embossed Tree Ornaments
Glitter Fruit
Keepsake Silver Bird Ornament
Gingerbread Birdhouses
Bath Oil
Meringue Mushrooms

MARY NEWELL DEPALMA:
Reversible Table Wreath
Crystal and Wire Ornaments
Beaded Star Ornaments
Hinged Angel Screen
Cuffed Velvet Stocking
Court Jester Stocking
Folded Paper Envelopes
Cut-Window Collage Cards
Zippered Suede Purses
Lined Velvet Pouches
Faux Brushed-Steel Frame

Photography:

All photographs in this book were taken by **CARL TREMBLAY** with the following exceptions: Della Robbia Wreath; Evergreen, Roses, and Lime Wreath; Gingerbread Birdhouses; Lined Velvet Pouches; and Cuffed Velvet Stocking by **STEVEN MAYS.**

Patterns:

ROBERTA FRAUWIRTH

Index

angel gift tag **134**

angel screen, hinged **74–77**

animals, stuffed **174–178, 187**

appliquéd wool stocking **78–83, 181**

artificial flowers, foliage, and fruits

Della Robbia wreath **18–21**

glitter ornaments **62–67**

reversible table wreath **28**

white silk rose wreath **10–13**

art supplies, sources for **188–189**

autumnal stocking **82**

baskets, gold leafed **96**

bath oil **138–141**

beaded candle holder **166–169**

beaded star ornaments **52–57**

birdhouses, gingerbread **98–103, 187**

bird ornament, silver **68–71**

blanket stitch **81, 82, 83**

books, miniature **142–145, 186**

boxes

gold leafed **96**

pavé **150–153**

brass fittings

hinged angel screen **76, 77**

pavé boxes **152, 153**

broken gold leafing technique **96**

brushed-steel frame, faux **162–165**

bunny, stuffed **175–176, 177, 187**

buttonhole stitch *see blanket stitch*

candle holder, beaded **166–169**

candle making supplies, sources for **188**

candles, gilded **94–97**

cathedral and church, miniature **90, 92, 93, 182, 183**

collage cards, cut-window **112–115**

colors, for holiday decorations **86**

composition leaf **96**

cookery projects

decorative baking goods, sources for **188**

gingerbread birdhouses **98–103, 187**

meringue mushrooms **146–149**

cottage, miniature **90, 91, 92, 184**

couching **83**

court jester stocking **104–109, 185**

craft supplies, sources for **188–189**

crystal and wire ornaments **48–51**

cuffed velvet stocking **84–87, 186**

custom-fit teddy bear sweaters **170–173**

cut-window collage cards **112–115**

decorative baking goods, sources for **188**

decoupage

glass ornaments **33, 34, 35**

hinged angel screen **74–77**

Della Robbia wreath **18–21**

door wreath **14–17**

dried flowers, herbs, and foliage

for bath oils **140**

for reversible table wreath **27**

embossing

cut-window collage cards **114**

fruit and vegetable ornaments **38–43, 180**

glass ball ornaments **37**

glitter balls **45, 46, 47**

laminated greeting cards **126, 127**

rubber stamp gift tags **134, 135**

embroidery

appliquéd stocking **79, 81–82**

decorative stitches **83**

terry cloth animals **176, 178**

Empire-style door wreath **14–17**

envelopes

for flat gifts **116–119**

for greeting cards **115, 123**

evergreen, rose, and lime wreath **22–25**

evergreens **12**

fresh, for wreath **24, 25**

miniature, for gilded village **91**

faux brushed-steel frame **162–165**

floral foods **24**

floral supplies, sources for **189**

flowers and foliage, artificial *see artificial flowers, foliage, and fruits*

flowers and foliage, dried *see dried flowers, herbs, and foliage*

fresh evergreen, rose and lime wreath **23, 24, 25**

hydration of **24**

reversible table wreath **27, 28**

folded paper envelopes **116–119**

frames

faux brushed-steel **162–165**

wooden, for table wreath **27, 28, 29**

fruit and vegetable ornaments

embossed **38–43, 180**

glitter fruits and vegetables **62–67**

fruits, artificial *see artificial flowers, foliage, and fruits*

gift tags **111**

rubber stamp **132–135**

gilded candles **94–97**

gilded glitter village **88–93, 182–184**

gingerbread birdhouses **98–103, 187**

glass ball ornaments **32–37**

glitter balls **44–47**

gold leafing **96**

glitter

balls **44–47**

fruit **62–67**
 gilded village **88–93, 182–184**
 Moravian stars **58–61, 180**
 sizes and shapes of **67**
gold leafing
 gilded candles **95–97**
 glass ball ornaments **34, 35, 96**
greeting cards **110–131**
handmade gifts **136–178**
hardwood frame **164**
herbal supplies, sources for **189**
herbs, dried *see dried flowers, herbs, and foliage*
hinged angel screen **74–77**
house, miniature **90, 91, 93, 184**
image bank **130**
keepsake silver bird ornament **68–71**
knitted teddy bear sweaters **170–173**
labels, for bath oil **140**
laminated greeting cards **124–127**
lime, rose, and evergreen wreath **22–25**
lined velvet pouches **158–161**
mantel decorations **72–109**
mat, picture frame **164–165**
meringue mushrooms **146–149**
miniature notepad books **142–145, 186**
Moravian glitter stars **58–61, 180**
Murano glass-style stocking **82**
nineteenth-century stocking **82**
notepad books **142–145, 186**
ornaments **30–71**
paper projects
 cut-window cards **112–115**
 folded paper envelopes **116–119**
 laminated greeting cards **124–127**
 notepad books **142–145, 186**
 rubber stamp gift tags **132–135**
 Scotty dog card **120–123, 187**
 stationery greeting cards **128–131**

 supplies, sources for **189**
patterns **180–187**
pavé box **150–153**
piglet, stuffed **175–178, 187**
pinecones
 Della Robbia wreath **20**
 gift tag **134, 135**
pine frame **164**
plastic cherubs, gold leafed **96**
plastic fruit
 glitter fruit **63–67**
 gold leafing **96**
plastic needlepoint canvas **90, 91**
pliers, types of **169**
pour-in-paint ornament **33, 36**
puppy, stuffed **178**
purses and pouches
 lined velvet pouches **158–161**
 zippered suede purse **154–157**
remnants, fabric **161**
retro-style stocking **82**
reverse-stencil ornaments **33, 37**
reversible table wreath **26–29**
rose window **90, 93**
rose wreaths **10–13, 22–25**
rubber stamps
 gift tags **132–135**
 greeting cards **126, 127**
Saturnalia **12**
Scotty dog holiday card **120–123, 187**
screen, hinged **74–77**
sewing projects
 appliquéd stocking **78–83, 181**
 court jester stocking **104–109, 185**
 cuffed stocking **84–87, 186**
 suede purse **154–157**
 supplies, sources for **189**
 terry cloth animals **174–178, 187**
 velvet pouches **158–161**
silk foliage **19, 20,**
silk rose wreath **10–13**
silver bird ornament **68–71**

silver leafing kit **70**
size (glue) **96**
star gift tag **134**
star ornaments
 beaded **52–57**
 Moravian **58–61, 180**
stationery greeting cards **128–131**
stockings
 appliquéd wool **78–83, 181**
 court jester **104–109, 185**
 cuffed velvet **84–87, 186**
stuffed animals **174–178, 187**
suede book covers **143, 144, 145**
suede purses **154–157**
sweaters, teddy bear **170–173**
table wreath, reversible **26–29**
teddy bear sweaters **170–173**
terry cloth animals **174–178, 187**
ultrasuede book covers **144**
vegetable and fruit ornaments *see fruit and vegetable ornaments*
velveteen covered mat **165**
velvet pouches **158–161**
velvet stocking, cuffed **84–87, 186**
village, gilded glitter **88–93, 182–184**
white rose wreath **10–13**
whitewash **153**
windows, for miniature buildings **90, 91, 93**
wire and crystal ornaments **48–51**
woodworking projects
 hinged angel screen **74–77**
 table wreath frame **27, 28, 29**
wool
 appliquéd stocking **78–83, 181**
 boiling and shrinking **80**
 dyeing **82**
wreaths **8–29**
 history of **12**
zippered suede purses **154–157**